LIVING
WONDERFULLY

By the same author:
Laughter, the Best Medicine
Stress Busters
What Number Are You? (with Lilla Bek)

LIVING
WONDERFULLY

A Joyful Guide to
Conscious–Creative Living

Robert Holden

Thorsons
An Imprint of HarperCollins*Publishers*

The Aquarian Press
An Imprint of HarperCollins*Publishers*
77–85 Fulham Palace Road,
Hammersmith, London W6 8JB
1160 Battery Street,
San Francisco, California 94111–1213

Published by Aquarian Press 1994
3 5 7 10 8 6 4 2

A catalogue record for this book
is available from the British Library

ISBN 1 85538 351 9

Printed and bound in Great Britain by
HarperCollinsManufacturing Glasgow

I dedicate this book to the
Glory of God.

Beloved Miranda, accept this book
as a gift of love and gratitude.
Being with you is, truly, wonder-full!
I love you.

Oh Divine Creator of all this Wonder,
I pray that You bathe this beautiful
World with Your Light, Your Love
and Your Laughter.
May Your Light inspire and uplift my mind.
May Your Love touch and open up my heart.
May Your Laughter free and renew my body.
I drink in Your Wonder so that every perception,
every thought, every belief, every word
and every action be blessed.
Grant me every opportunity, this day, to be a joyful
emissary, a wise counsel and a holy fool! Let
me add to this wonder-full Creation.
Let there be Light. Let there be Love. Let
there be Laughter!

CONTENTS

ACKNOWLEDGEMENTS

From the very first moment I got the idea for a book called 'Living Wonder-fully' I became so excited the whole of my body shook for nearly 36 hours. The 4,000-word synopsis was complete within about three hours—it just poured out. I was fully charged, my whole being was electric, I couldn't rest and I couldn't sleep—the only way I could cope was to go to the supermarket!

Ever since I got the idea for this book, truly wonder-full things have happened in my life. Perhaps the truth is that wonder-full things happen all the time, It's just that I am now more aware, more appreciative. The most wonder-full happening has been my marriage to Miranda—I met Miranda four days after I wrote my synopsis!

The greatest privilege in life is being able to say 'thank you' to people you love and value. Many people have helped me to put *Living Wonderfully* together. Thank you, first, to Sally my mum, David my brother and all of my inspirational friends. Thank you, also, to our two cats, called Wonderful and Great—they are two little miracles who always have another point of view!

Thank you to Michelle Hope for your excellent research for 'miracles'. Thank you to my assistant, Carol

Stevens, for all your marvellous help and support. Thank you, once again, to my consultant editor and friend Erica Smith, whose encouragement and help are so very much appreciated. And thank you to Barbara Vesey for your thorough work on editing and improving the text. *Living Wonderfully* has been a truly wonder-full experience!

1

WONDER

MIRACLES

Why, who makes much of a miracle?
As to me I know of nothing else but miracles,
Whether I walk the streets of Manhattan,
Or dart my sight over the roofs of houses toward the sky,
Or wade with naked feet along the beach just in the
    edge of the water,
Or stand under the trees in the woods,
Or talk by day with any one I love, or sleep in the bed
    at night with any one I love,
Or sit at table at dinner with the rest,
Or look at strangers opposite me riding in the car,
Or watch honey-bees busy around the hive of a summer forenoon,
Or animals feeding in the fields,
Or birds, or the wonderfulness of insects in the air,
Or the wonderfulness of the sundown, or of stars
    shining so quiet and bright,
Or the exquisite delicate thin curve of the new moon in spring;
These with the rest, one and all, are to me miracles,
The whole referring, yet each distinct and in its place.
To me every hour of the light and dark is a miracle,
Every cubic inch of space is a miracle,
Every square yard of the surface of the earth is spread with the same,
Every foot of the interior swarms with the same,
To me the sea is a continual miracle,
The fishes that swim—the rocks—the motion of the waves
    —the ships with men in them,
What stranger miracles are there?'

Walt Whitman

To wonder is natural—we live, after all, in a world that is so odd, bizarre and amazing; everything in it is a total surprise. When I allow my Self to stop and think and feel and see and be with life, my heart grows almost too big for my body. Why should there be green grass, I wonder? How does a tulip become red, yellow, white or pink? Why do birds sing together at dawn? What makes the wind blow? Why are there cucumbers, amethysts and plums? What magic! What mystery! What miracles!

When I shift from human *doing* to human *being*, I am amazed even at my own life and existence. I, too, share the feelings of the wonder-full Indian poet and mystic, Rabindrath Tagore, who wrote, 'That I exist is a perpetual surprise which is life.' Where have I come from? What made me? Why am I here? What is my purpose? How do I live and grow? Why do I have hands and feet? Not even the scientists can give me a complete explanation of how I am able to wiggle my little finger.

Wonder inspires joy, reverence, gratitude and thanksgiving. Living 'wonder-fully' encourages us, day by day, to live consciously and creatively, to be even more unconditionally in tune and in harmony with whatever is happening than ever before.

Alas, our inner aliveness, or 'wonder-power', is so often dampened by work, worry and woe that we may go for hours, weeks, months and even years before we make time again to wonder a while at life. We spend so much time as *human doings* and so little as *human beings* that we lose sight of the privilege, the miracle of being alive. Sadly, we also lose sight of our own miraculous potential for growth, happiness and transcendence.

Let's face it: life is a total bonus, this solar system is a good option, and existence is a pretty marvellous deal—it certainly beats non-existence! Thank 'God' for life! Please note that whenever I mention that three-letter word, 'God', I am not thinking of a grouchy, judgmental old man or woman who patrols the skies, with one home in this solar system, an office in the neighbouring galaxy and a villa someplace else in the Milky Way. Rather, I think of 'God' as a *universal, creative Intelligence* which has initiated and supports the whole caboodle—beetles and bugs, panda bears, four-leaf clovers, pot plants, icebergs, shooting stars, planets, solar systems, the lot. 'God' isn't just on the outside; 'God' is inside, too—the universal, creative Intelligence is inside each of us. I use the word 'Intelligence' with a capital 'I' because creation is the most Intelligent thing I have ever witnessed.

WONDERING

When was the last time you wondered around the planet? We live on a beautiful blue-green planet over-flowing with so many brilliant, flourishing examples of life, beauty, creativity, strength and accomplishment. I cannot help but feel that each example is a testimony to our own wonder-full potential. The Earth, her Self, is a veritable goddess. How the Earth was formed remains a mystery—we can only guess at her genesis. Scientists estimate she is about 4,500 million years old—which makes her a young whipper-snapper compared to many other planets in the universe.

Wonder at this: 45,000 thunderstorms occur every day around the world; a lightning bolt has an average temperature of 34,000°C; over 3,000 earthquakes happen every year on Earth; the Pacific Ocean covers 180 million square km; one in five km of the Earth is arid desert; Mother Earth has well over 500,000 lakes and over 100,000 rivers, the longest of which is the Nile (over 660 km).

Mother Earth supports over 4 million different species of life. Imagine! We share this world with over 4 million other different families. The skies of Earth are populated by nearly 10,000 species of bird. The average duck travels up to 1500 km a day during migration; the biggest bird of all, the ostrich, cannot fly but it can run at up to 50 km an hour.

Back down on the ground, the common garden spider has over 500 silk glands and can lay up to 500 eggs at a time; crickets hear through their knees; there is a brown butterfly in Brazil that smells of chocolate; caterpillars are propelled by over two thousand muscles (1400 more muscles than humans); scientists have found a breed of flea in Germany that only lives and breeds inside beer mats; a midge can flap its wings up to 2,100 times a second; a flea can jump to up to 350 times its own height; and paper wasps invented paper thousands of years before humans got around to making it.

And what of the ocean life? Over 20,000 species of fish swim the seas of Earth. Some species of deep sea fish produce their own light to see by; sea urchins walk on their teeth; and the butterfly fish has tail markings that resemble Arabic script which translates as, 'There is no God but Allah'!

There are thousands of amazing mammals on Mother Earth, like the humpback whale whose song can carry over 30 km and the cheetah who can accelerate from 0 to 72 km an hour in less than three seconds. Many mammals have 'super senses' of smell, taste, sight and hearing that far excel human standards.

And then there is the astonishing, prolific world of plants, foliage and vegetables. Thomas Carlyle got it right when he wrote, 'This world, after all our science and sciences, is still a miracle; wonderful, inscrutable, magical and more, to whosoever will think of it.' Life is a naturally occurring miracle, and we are each of us a part of this miracle.

YOUR MIRACULOUS POTENTIAL

Two things fill the mind with ever new and increasing wonder and awe—the starry heavens above me, and the moral law with me.

Immanuel Kant

'We carry within us the wonders we seek without us,' wrote the English physician, Sir Thomas Browne. Take a look at your own body. The body is the result of many millions of years of work carried out by the universal, creative Intelligence. It is estimated that the first cell took 1,100 million years to create—after that everything appears to have been comparatively plain sailing. Today, in the next hour, for example, your body will produce approximately 9,000 million red blood cells. Your heart pumps approximately 13 tons (3,000 gallons) of blood around your body every day. Because the heart rests between beats, in an average lifetime of 70 years the heart can rest for a total of 40 years. You have over 600 muscles in your body, each working in perfect harmony with the others so as to co-ordinate walking, running, jumping, dancing and simply standing still. The smallest muscle of all is the *stapedius*, only 1 mm long—without it you might find it difficult to hear.

The brain is made up of approximately 12,000 million cells. The fastest nerve impulses in the body travel at up to 300 km an hour. The tongue has over 10,000 taste buds. Most of our long bones are lighter and stronger than reinforced concrete. There are over 130 million light receptors in the retina, and the eyes will focus an estimated 100,000 times a day. Adult males produce over 100 million sperm each day. We even sneeze on average at 150 km an hour!

As amazing as all this is, we are more than a body: we are thought, feeling, emotion, intuition, imagination, creativity and spirit. The universal, creative Intelligence courses through our veins; we are plugged in to universal potentials. Each of us tends a wonder-full inner garden where seeds of creative aliveness can take root and eventually blossom. We are a product of the laws of universal life, and these laws are based on abundance. There is no shortage of potential, no limit to possibilities and no maximum point of growth. And deep within us there is what metaphysician Sir George King coined 'a miracle kit'. In other words, you have the potential to create 'wonder-full' things in your life, be they at play, at work, with art, in education, with family and in relationships. Part of the art of living wonderfully is knowing how to tap this potential and then use it for the maximum good of all of us.

MIRACLE CONSCIOUSNESS

> True Miracles are created by men [and women] when they
> use the courage and intelligence that God gave them.
>
> *Jean Anouilh*

'We are hemmed round with mystery, and the greatest mysteries are contained in what we see and do every day,' wrote Henri Frédéric Amiel. The more you notice, the more there is to notice. By becoming increasingly conscious of the miracles that are forever happening around you, the more aware you can become of the potential miracles that are forever possible within you. This is *miracle consciousness*.

Miracle Consciousness describes the living, dynamic, everlasting process of owning, opening up to and realizing your innate potential. Miracle consciousness is a way of seeing, believing, thinking, communicating and acting. It is an attitude, a way of being that is conscious–creative, playful, loving and expansive. The potential for wonder exists around you and in you—right now! Once you know what you want, the next task is to find out what can help to bring it about.

Miracle consciousness is based on seven imaginative insights:

1. *Life is miraculous!*
   There is a magic, a mystery and a miracle to everything. Your existence is a miracle that no one can fully explain. Resolve, therefore, to make the most of this miracle: play, explore, venture, investigate and experiment with life. Be conscious, be creative, be courageous and be full of wonder.

2. *You are a miracle!*
'What lies behind us and what lies before us are tiny
matters compared to what lies within us,' wrote the
American poet Ralph Waldo Emerson. You are a child
of the evolving miracle called creation. Your potential
is a universal river that never runs dry.

3. *This is the age of miracles!*
Now, today, is the time for a wonderful new beginning;
now is the time for a fresh start; and *now* is the time for
a different way of being. Too often we defer and delay
our happiness, our joy and our fulfilment: we are always
preparing to live but often end up putting it off. 'One
of these days' is usually 'none of these days'. Living
wonderfully is all about now or never, today or no day!

4. *You can make a miracle happen!*
Don't wait for a miracle to happen *to you*; go out and
make a miracle happen *through you*. If today you are
waiting for life to happen to you, you will find that
tomorrow you will still be waiting. Life is a conscious-
creative act—you have the power to create and re-create
again and again. Of all the influences that shape your
life, you are the biggest influence and you have the last
word. Take responsibility for your Self. Courage is the
first freedom.

5. *Miracles, luck and good fortune*
Has life a purpose? Is existence by design or by default?
At some point in your life you must decide whether or
not you are going to believe in and live by luck. Will
you wait for luck or go out and build your own good
fortune? As Benjamin Disraeli put it, 'Man is not the
creature of circumstances; circumstances are the
creatures of men.'

6. *Miracles and the impossible*
   'Impossible—that's not good French!' quipped
   Napoleon. So often personal growth and happiness are
   thwarted and denied by the cry of 'Impossible!' When
   we feel unhappy, happiness can certainly seem
   impossible; in truth, though, this feeling is a fiction,
   not a fact. Change your outlook and the way things
   look will change also. Most miracles are merely
   courage, perseverance and energy in disguise.

7. *Miracles are for ever.*
   Every moment in time holds an eternal potential for
   greater living. There are no ordinary moments. Hold on
   to the magic, the mystery and the miracle and, as the
   ancient Sioux Indian saying goes, 'May the Great
   Mystery make sunrise in your heart today.'

BIRTH

Man's main task in life is to give birth to himself, to become what he potentially is.

Erich Fromm

Perhaps the greatest miracle of all is the birth of a beautiful child—and all children are beautiful. The whole event, from conception to delivery, is one of the most awe-inspiring experiences of all existence. Take one ovum, add one sperm and, over a short passage of time, a baby is born with a unique, original, one-off combination of genes the like of which the world has never known nor will ever know again.

Each baby is a fresh, beautiful blossom planted on Earth for the purpose of unfolding, flowering and achieving a unique fruition. The poet Lord Byron described a new-born child as, 'a rose with all its sweetest leaves yet unfolded'. Without even trying, we are each of us totally unique—with talents, skills, characteristics, ideas, perceptions and contributions waiting to bud and to blossom.

Each new-born child is as a link between spirit and matter, Heaven and Earth, angels and humanity. Babies are our angels, our Heaven and our sweet inspiration. We were all that way once; a part of us will be that way for ever. We are forever born. If you have a photograph of your Self as a new-born child or a young infant, carry it with you always.

REBIRTH AND RECREATION

Become aware of what is in you. Announce it, pronounce it, produce it and give birth to it.

Meister Eckhart

After the miracle of physical birth is over, we also experience throughout life the birth of wonder and awareness, of emotion and feeling, intuition and creativity, intellect and logic, skill and talent. Friendships are born, relationships are born and we, too, may experience the birth of our own beautiful children. Birth is a lifelong process.

Birth, change and evolution are the essence of life— nothing much retains its original form for long. One day we contract; another day we expand. Every day we can give birth to a new thought, a new feeling, a new belief, a new action, a new idea and a new reality. A conscious–creative awareness means we are forever giving birth to our Self.

Today is new—it has never happened before! Today is, therefore, the ideal time for a new beginning, a fresh start, a lively enterprise, a creative chapter, even a metamorphosis. 'Be ye transformed by the renewing of your mind,' (Romans 12:12). Birth is not only wonderful, it is also highly courageous—stepping into the unknown, the unpredictable and the unforeseen. Opportunities exist for everyone; with courage, we can *make* even more

13

opportunities than we find.

'The living self has one purpose only,' wrote D. H. Lawrence, 'to come into its own fullness of being, as a tree comes into full blossom, or a bird into spring beauty, or a tiger into lustre.' Each of us has what one mystic called 'a divine itch' to bring into being our inner, universal creative potential. Deep within us all there is an urge to deliver, contribute and be all that we are. We each need to plant our tree—for our Self, for our 'God' and for all humanity.

To give birth to the real Self is the ultimate act of love in life. To be all that we are and to become all that we might be is the joyful challenge set before each and every one of us. Being our Self is the wisest philosophy, the bravest action, the kindest consideration and the greatest act of healing imaginable. To be real is to set your Self free—and finding your own freedom is also the greatest gift and inspiration you can give to your family, friends and fellow travellers.

'The ultimate import of our human birth is to discover or realize the truth of our life. To do so, however, we are required to observe, understand, and transcend ourselves,' wrote John White, editor of *What is Enlightenment?* (Aquarian Press, 1984). To contact, incarnate and live in the light of a higher Self and a higher potential are the perennial themes of terrestrial psychology, religion and philosophy. First we must give birth to an individual consciousness in which we live in harmony with our Self; thereafter, we must give birth to a cosmic consciousness in which we are citizens of the universe living in harmony with everything.

'No single event can awaken within us a stranger

totally unknown to us. To live is to be slowly born,' said the writer Antoine de Saint Exupéry. To live a life filled with wonder it is essential to realize that life is an eternal process of birth upon birth upon birth—even the experience called 'death' may, in truth, be the beginning of another journey through a another sort of birth canal. Now that you are born, you can give birth to your Self and to the life-potential within you—this is living wonderfully.

THE WONDER-CHILD

Wonder is especially proper to childhood, and it is the sense of wonder above all that keeps us young.

Gerald Vann

In the beginning, everything is a source of wonder! A child will naturally fill the day with unconditional awe, everlasting energy, ceaseless curiosity, a tireless penchant for play, a continual desire to communicate, an abundance of creative fun and an ever-evolving expression of love. When we watch children we are reminded of our own birthright—we can and should take this birthright into adulthood with us!

I love the words of Mary Howitt, who once observed:

God sends children for another purpose than merely to keep up the race—to enlarge our hearts; and to make us unselfish and full of kindly sympathies and affections; to give our souls higher aims; to call out all our facilities to extended enterprise and exertion; and to bring round our firesides bright faces, happy smiles, and loving, tender hearts. My soul blesses the great Father, every day, that he has gladdened the Earth with little children.

Traditionally, a child is a symbol of enlightenment in the Christian, Buddhist, Taoist, Hindu and Islamic faiths. 'Verily I say unto you, whosoever shall not receive the kingdom of God as a little child, he shall not enter therein,' (Luke 21:23). I also love the words of J.R. Lovell, who wrote, 'Children are God's apostles, sent forth, day by day, to preach of love and hope and peace.'

The child is eternal—it never dies. Each of us carries a unique 'wonder child' within us—it is at play in your heart at this very moment if you can *feel* it. We are none of us old really; in truth, we are eternally young. 'A person is always startled when he hears himself seriously called old for the first time,' wrote the American physician Oliver Wendell Holmes. The 'wonder-child' is forever young, forever newly arrived and forever just born.

Alas, it is to our great detriment that as a society we fail to champion our children. These young miracles—pure expressions of the universal, creative Intelligence—find themselves not in a 'wonder-full' world but a sad, sorry, suffering society in which they are soon taught to grow up and shut up, be seen and not heard, be 'sensible, not silly', and to 'act like adults'. No wonder so many adults soon lose communication with their own inner child.

The modern medical professional describes a pregnant woman as a 'patient' who has a 'condition'. It is as if pregnancy were an illness! Unnatural birth methods mean that mother—and child—are often pumped with foreign, artificial chemicals during labour; the infant is often dragged out of the birth canal with cold metal instruments, from the warmth and liquid darkness of the womb into a cold, harshly lit hospital room; and the umbilical cord is cut before the child has learned to breathe for him- or her Self.

What a welcome! Our children are introduced, immediately, to fear, to upset and to tears. Many people act as if the child is not intelligent enough to feel at all, nor to be emotionally scared, to hold a grudge, or even to remember any of it. I can vividly remember my birth— many people do. I was so indignant! The memory of physical birth is stored in our bodies, in our hearts and in our minds.

Thankfully, psychotherapeutic techniques such as rebirthing, vivation and primal integration therapy, for instance, acknowledge that birth trauma is a very real fact that can haunt a person throughout his or her adult life. Also, active birth methods such as underwater birth are now evolving and gaining respect for the professional, caring way in which they attune themselves, often intuitively, to the sensitive requirements of each beautiful wonder-child.

It is time, I believe, for you and I to champion our children today as never before—it is also time, today, to reclaim our own inner wonder-child. We must not leave this child behind; we must, if we want to blossom and mature, take the wonder-child with us, giving our Self full permission to play, to be creative, to risk once more. The adult is the student, the child the teacher—we must be humble enough to learn.

ALIVENESS

Youth smiles without reason. It is one of its chiefest charms.

Oscar Wilde

For the new-born child, life flows freely—there are few blocks, barriers or buts, and thus, laughter, tears, trust and love all flow freely. Free-flowing expression is natural to a new-born child, who has yet to learn the adult devices of suppression, repression, denial, resistance and fear.

Young children bring an energy, animation, vitality, spirit and zest to almost everything they do. Give a child a wooden spoon and it soon becomes a drumstick, a paddle, a portable phone, a pair of binoculars, a walking stick— and a wooden spoon, of course! Children possess creativity and *aliveness* in abundance; this is the secret of their energy. Alas, poor, tired parents can rarely keep up, for the energy of an average adult is stale and stagnant by comparison.

We must not lose our aliveness. 'The young are permanently in a state resembling intoxication: for youth is sweet and they are growing,' said Aristotle. The aliveness of a young child is as divine inebriation compared to the average sombre sobriety of adulthood. Yet for most of us, what was once a raging fire is now only a spark—the 'wonder-child' plays on but it is rarely seen or heard. 'The tragedy of life is what dies inside a man while he lives,' wrote Albert Schweitzer.

The secret of life is: life! The challenge set before us is not to exist only, but to be alive fully. Unconditional life! We must embrace the lot—laughter and tears, happiness and sorrow, pleasure and pain. Throughout the years our primary task is to give birth to spirit in matter—we are here to energize and spiritualize everything. With constant intention, the right tools and sufficient aliveness we can integrate and make peace with everything, including (starting with, more like) our Self. Let the adventure begin!

ADVENTURE

Life is either a daring adventure or nothing. To keep our faces towards change and behave like free spirits in the presence of fate is strength undefeatable.

Helen Keller

Each and every day of life we are blessed with another 24 hours of potential new experience, for none of us has 'done' today before. Today is, therefore, an experiment during which we can make and receive opportunities, openings and occasions to walk, skip, dance, unfold and evolve with life. Today is your invitation to live.

With each sunrise, countless opportunities can also be made to live, love, laugh and learn. We are explorers, making two journeys in life: an outer journey in which we discover and open out to the world of wonders around us, and an inner journey in which we locate and look into a treasure chest of glittering assets and golden potentials. Ours is a spiritual odyssey. The adventure is always ready to begin again for those of us who are willing to live 'wonder-fully'.

LIFE AND DEATH

Let us endeavour so to live that when we come to die even the undertaker will be sorry.

Mark Twain

I firmly believe that human beings are happiness-orientated and joy-directed. Almost every human action, intuition and behaviour is influenced in some way by a deep desire for ever-evolving happiness and everlasting joy. Experiences of *true* happiness, *real* joy and *inner* fulfilment are among our primary goals in life. Today is, for most of us, an adventure and a search for the experience of a more real happiness than we found yesterday.

Happiness is easy when we are full of wonder, for wonder is a form of worship that makes us aware of our blessings. When we are unconditional with wonder it is easy to be happy—we like our Self because we 'are'; we love life because it 'is'; and we are happy just to 'be'. Life is a blessing. The fewer conditions that exist, the greater the chance for happiness. It is all very simple—until, that is, we get hurt.

Whenever we are hurt in life, our ego wants to defend and protect us. We experience a great temptation to create conditions, build barriers and shut down for safety. 'I won't be happy again until I can be sure I won't be hurt,' one person cries; 'I'm not going to get involved again,' promises another; and, 'That's the last time,' threatens a third. Too often, in their efforts to block out future hurt people also end up blocking out future happiness.

So often in my own psychotherapy practice I listen to people's inner dilemma of whether or not to open up to life again: 'If I shut my Self away I won't be happy, but at least I won't feel such pain again,' they reason. This is a bit like saying, 'I'll deal with life by pretending to be dead'! This unhappy compromise does not create an absence of hurt; on the contrary, it creates more hurt the longer the compromise goes on.

In my 'Living Wonder-fully' seminars, participants are asked to create a personal philosophy that actually embraces both happiness and hurt. The fact is, hurt exists; do not deny it. Own your hurt; allow it to help you. Express it; don't suppress it. Every hurt is a help if you can see why. Don't fight or struggle; make peace with your hurt. Hurt is not good or bad in itself—it is what we do with it that makes it one or the other. In every hurt there is another opportunity for greater happiness (see Part III: 'Rainbows').

Where there is hurt the ego can become so hooked and attached to the experience of pain that perceptions, thoughts and belief systems develop that invite more pain: we may start to 'see' pain as unavoidable, to 'think' pain follows pleasure, and to 'believe' we deserve to suffer today—particularly if yesterday went well! And so we create a life and a philosophy that not only makes pain and suffering inevitable but even somehow tries to glorify them.

Unless we make peace with our hurt and our pain, *fear of life* will prevail over *love of life*. The urge to 'play dead', to close off and to shut down will win over the 'divine itch' to come alive again, open up and venture forth once more. Fear is bondage; bravery offers freedom. And, as Helen Keller once said, 'Avoiding danger [fear] is no safer in the long run than outright exposure [life]. The fearful are caught as often as the bold.'

The great medication we all long for is *fulfilment through quality of life*. To achieve this we must continue always to live, not die. Our life adventure demands that we embrace and work with—not against—the hurt, pain and fear we may meet along the way, and still choose to live. Hurt, pain and fear can be used to create favourable outcomes. Do not postpone your life: the happiness of life does not happen in the future; it happens *now*. The adventure is *now*.

THE UNFOLDING DRAMA

Sometimes even to live is an act of courage.

Seneca

Life isn't something that just happens *to* you; you can make your life happen *for* you. Alas, those who wait for life to happen to them are often left waiting; those who work at life are often healthier, happier and more whole. When it comes to your own life you are not an audience, you are an actor, and more.

Life is an unfolding drama in which you can add to your own script through the perceptions, thoughts, beliefs, words and actions you own. You can also edit, direct, produce and stage-manage your life at any time by exercising your most potent power: the power of *choice*. No one day, event or single experience is implicitly 'good' or 'bad', 'great' or 'gruelling', 'liberating' or 'limiting'—*choosing* makes it so. Life is the choice you make of it.

Today, you can choose how to 'be'. Choice is an internal power—by choosing how to think, feel and live inside the Self, we are also choosing directly how life shall be outside and around us. The climate within affects and alters the climate without. Our inner world is the *cause* which creates the outer world of *effect*. Today, you can choose to recreate an old yesterday or invent a new tomorrow—the creative power of choice is yours for ever.

'The art of living rightly is like all arts: it must be learned and practised with incessant care,' wrote Goethe. Living 'wonder-fully' is an art—it is also a highly adaptable talent that needs to be polished and refined constantly. Living 'wonder-fully' is a creative adventure which challenges constantly our inner resources of choice, will, adaptability and aliveness.

In a workshop I facilitate entitled *Invent Your Self!*, participants take time and space to experience the living power of adventure that exists both inside and outside themselves. You might like to play with the following 10 themes of the adventure park we commonly call *life!*

Experimentation

Experiment with today, for today has never ever happened before in the whole history of the universe. Experiment with your Self, for you have a potential that is as deep, high and wide as you want to make it. When it comes to potential, *you have to try it out to help bring it out.* Experimentation yields results. 'Do not be too timid and squeamish about your actions. All life is an experiment,' wrote Emerson.

Innovation

No two days are ever the same: yesterday was unlike today; today is unlike tomorrow. Hurt, pain and fear often encourage us to resist the inevitable. How proud some people are when they tell you of a friend: 'Good old John—I've known him for 50 years and he hasn't changed a bit.' Poor old John—how sad! The joy of life is not staying the same, but evolving, transforming and transforming again. Change, by choice, is the evidence of growth.

Invention

'To be nobody-but-myself—in a world which is doing its best, night and day, to make you everybody else—means to fight the hardest battle which any human being can fight, and never stop fighting,' said the poet e.e. cummings. Ultimately we are our own role models, our own inspiration, for no one else has our unique, individual potential. Invent your Self! Take a trait, characteristic or frame of mind, such as optimism for example, and invent it in your Self. Make your own magic; practise it and it will become real.

Discovery

Dining out with my younger brother David is a wonderful education. He is always popular, generous, cordial and exceptionally quick to know what he wants to eat. He knows what he likes—because he doesn't like anything he hasn't tried! Sometimes, in life, people restrict themselves this way. A part of the fun of adventure is to go where you have never gone before—that way you create the possibility of joyful discovery. Try something new on the menu today!

Risk

'Behold the turtle; he makes progress only when he sticks his neck out,' quipped James Bryant Conant. In order to receive, we must give. By giving of our Self we risk failure, rejection and upset; by not giving of our Self we guarantee failure, rejection and upset. Brave actions inspire bravery. Risk and you can receive. Make joy of all you gain; make light of all you lose.

Enter-prize

For several years now I have been privileged to hold a small counselling practice for staff of the BBC. One of my clients, whom I will call Claire, was stuck: life was not going well and she was waiting for things to get better. She had struck up a deal with life: give me something great and I'll come out to play again! She often talked about winning the football pools—not a million pounds, just a few thousand! At the beginning of session seven or so I asked her, 'How did the pools go this week?' 'What?' she asked. 'Did you win money?' I prompted. 'Oh no, I'd love to win, but I never actually enter!' she replied. You must enter if you want the prize.

Action

Anxiety or action? Anxiety has never once in the whole history of the human race ever solved a problem, eluded a fear or won a prize. The universe only rewards action! 'It is in your act that you exist...Your act is your Self, and there is no other you,' wrote Saint Exupéry. Feel the anxiety, but act anyway. All good adventures are action-packed. Whatever you choose, act on it. Anxiety makes nightmares; action can create dreams.

Failure!

I once spent several months on the New York stock market working for an investment bank. During my time in New York I made friends with a 91-year-old man called Eurt who was still actively managing an office full of 300 brokers. I once asked him, 'What makes a success?' He replied, 'A failure,' then added, 'if you want to keep succeeding, you have to at least be prepared to keep failing.' Every time you fail, you learn; every time you learn, you create a chance to succeed. Adventure is all about making the most of your successes and your failures (see Part III: 'Success').

Saying 'Yes'

In my assertion workshops, which I call Assertive, I am, I focus a little on how to say 'No' and a lot on how to say 'Yes.' I believe we are more motivated by 'yes' than by 'no', more by gains than losses, starts than stops. If you want more personal space, for instance, say 'Yes' to personal space and act affirmatively. Being assertive is affirmative.

27

Try it for your Self and see what I mean: what do you want to say 'yes' to today?

The Crusade

Other than your Self, what do you believe in and what do you live for? To crusade for a cause bigger than your own individual life adds strength to your personal causes. Deep within us there is a cavalier who loves to defend justice, save the victims and support the poor. Service to others is all part of the collective human adventure. What philosophy do you promote? What ethics and morals do you support? What society do you serve? Who and what benefits by you? What is your crusade?

WONDER

O friend, awake, and sleep no more! The night is over and gone, would you lose your day also? You have slept for unnumbered ages; this morning will you not awake?

Rabindranath Tagore

The Buddha paused for a moment to draw a long, deep breath of life into his well-formed physical frame. There was silence. The Buddha was surrounded by adoring disciples, all of them eager to feed on a crumb of wisdom, inspiration or truth. 'Are you a God?' came a question; 'No,' replied the Buddha. 'Are you the son of God?' they wondered; 'No more than you are,' replied the Buddha. 'Are you an angel?' they enquired; 'No,' replied the Buddha. 'Are you a saint?' they asked; 'No,' replied the Buddha. 'What are you then?' they demanded; 'I am awake,' replied the Buddha.

To wonder is to wake up to the world of possibilities that exists within and about you. Curiosity, fascination, interest and intrigue are conscious–creative devices that unlock potential, energy, imagination and ideas. Life is a little bit like a savings account: the more you invest, the more interest you make. Invest in wonder!

Using wonder to wake up to your true Self is part of

the lifelong process of giving birth to your universal, creative potential. Every moment can be a waking moment in which you discover something new about the Self. There is a magic in every moment that is waiting to manifest. You are the magician. Be awake to the possibilities, and arise to the challenge.

BOREDOM!

Oh don't the days seem lank and long
When all goes right and nothing goes wrong,
And isn't your life extremely flat
With nothing whatever to grumble at!

Gilbert and Sullivan, Princess Ida

'Boredom is a medical emergency!' says the American doctor/clown Patch Adams. Boredom is not always terminal; it just feels like it. If ever you feel your Self coming down with a bout of boredom, hesitate not: spring to your feet, drink a long, cool glass of water, shake your Self a few times and deliver your Self, post-haste, to the intensive care unit of your local hospital. Plead with the medical staff to give you an immediate series of tests for blood-pressure, heart rate and evidence of breath.

Boredom, like any other sort of 'bug', has a tangible effect on the physical body. Medical research has discovered that chronic boredom, in particular, can either raise or reduce blood-pressure, speed up or slow down the heart rate, add to muscle tension, increase tension of the nervous system, slow the breath and alter the flow of the so-called 'energy hormones' such as adrenalin, noradrenalin and the endorphins.

Boredom is a collapsed state of consciousness that is both a symptom and cause of fatigue, imagination-immunity, low gratitude response, powerlessness, bottom-sores (from sitting around all day) and withdrawal from wonder. Boredom also contributes to memory failure: we forget, for instance, we share this world with 4 million different species of life; we forget we have a universal, creative potential to hand; and we forget that, ultimately, life is what we make it.

Boredom is peculiar to humans; no other species appears to suffer from it. Most often, a bout of boredom is a complaint in disguise. The complaint is: 'Life isn't happening to me!' The remedy is simple: get excited about 'nothing' happening, and you will be even more excited when 'something' starts to happen! Use the apparent 'nothingness' to start 'somethingness'. It takes life to live life: life is an everyday experience, not a once-in-a-while extravagance.

CREATIVITY

Nothing is poetical if plain daylight is not poetical; and no monster should amaze us if the normal man does not amaze.

G. K. Chesterton

Living is a conscious–creative act: we create our blessings; we create our boredom. Some of our reality is created by our parents, our schooling, our friends, our relationships and our work; but most of our reality is created by our own Self-image, our belief systems, our frame of mind and our quality of communication with our Self and the world around us. Whatever we are doing, every moment we are helping to create and shape our own reality. Every living moment is a creative moment.

'Reverie is the groundwork of creative imagination,' wrote Somerset Maugham. Wonder, curiosity and fascination help open up the treasure-house of universal, creative potential stored within us. 'If your daily life seems poor, do not blame it; blame yourself, tell yourself that you are not poet enough to call forth its riches,' said Rainer Maria Rilke.

Some people forget they are creative; others pretend or convince themselves that they have no inner inventive spark. Everyone is creative; everything has creativity. You help create your happiness and your misery—even the socks you wear today are a creative statement you make about you. Perhaps your most creative thought of all is that you are not creative!

WISDOM

It was through the feeling of wonder that men now and at first began to philosophize.

Aristotle

Wonder is the basis for all knowledge and inspiration. To be surprised, to wonder is to begin to know and to understand. Through wonder we can become aware; through awareness we can enlighten our Self. We tune in to our true Self and to the world around us through wonder and curiosity. Remember, high interest creates its own rich dividends.

'You will find something far greater in the woods than you will in books. Stones and trees will teach you what you can never learn from masters,' said St Bernard of Clairvaux. Wonder generates wisdom all by itself. Through wonder we can evolve our simple ego consciousness into a magnificent collective or cosmic consciousness in which we realize our true connection with every other manifestation of the universal, creative Intelligence on this planet.

Living 'wonder-fully' teaches us, curiosity serves to wake us up to our own cosmic potential. Daily curiosity about the Self helps to develop a greater Self-revelation and a truer Self-knowledge; with truer Self-knowledge we are ready to Self-realize even more. The more you wonder at your Self the more you will know your Self.

Wonder is also a form of worship. To wonder at the beauty, the strength or the mere existence of something is a form of prayer. Wonder is a natural blessing in that it generates gratitude and thankfulness and results in joy. Wonder teaches us to value—the more we value the Self the more valuable it becomes; the same is also true of the world around us.

The more interest you show in your Self, the more you will find there is to get interested about.

'WONDER-FULL'

The world will never starve for want of wonders; but only for want of wonder.

G. K. Chesterton

People come to *Living Wonder-fully* workshops for a whole host of reasons, most of which are inspired by a desire for a higher quality of life. People want to enjoy themselves more, to feel good about themselves, to enrich their relationships, to experience an ever-evolving quality of life, to make peace with their hurt and their stress, to set a clearer direction in life, to begin a new beginning every day and to create a real happiness and true fulfilment that can last.

Before we can live 'wonder-fully', it helps to be curious about the Self. At these workshops, therefore, I supply a list of questions, some of which I present below. These questions will help you attune to your Self—to plug into your universal, creative potential. You can light your Self up with wonder. More than that, I believe that the questions you ask of your Self are the questions that help to illuminate the whole wide 'wonder-full' world around you.

For What Am I Truly Grateful?

Do you know what you have? Take 10 minutes to write down anything and everything that you appreciate about life, e.g. 'I can see,' 'I can smell,' 'I can walk,' 'caramel and pecan ice cream'. Ask your Self, 'why do I appreciate these things?' Begin to understand your inner Self. The law of appreciation is simple: *whatever you appreciate, appreciates.* The more you express appreciation, the more you will find to appreciate. Practise this law and you will prove it.

What Do I Love about Life?

'What do you love most about your life?' I asked one client. He drew breath, about to speak, then paused and let the breath out again. He shifted his weight from left to right, scratched his brow and stared at his feet. 'I can tell you what I don't love about my life,' he said.

Human beings often have a much clearer idea of what

they loathe than what they love. Enjoy 10 minutes writing down everything you love, and why. Each and every day, love is the lesson, for L.I.F.E. is all about Love In Free Expression.

What Tickles Me?

What do you find funny, and why? Who gives you joy, and why? Where do you enjoy your true Self the most, and why? What do you laugh about, and why? Create the space for another 10 minutes of your life to investigate what tickles your funny bone. Laughter is a lotion that soothes and invigorates all the limbs of body, mind and soul. 'Man is fond of counting his troubles, but he does not count his joys. If he counted them up as he ought to, he would see that every lot has enough happiness provided for it,' wrote Dostoevsky.

What Nourishes Me?

What feeds your happiness? What fills your heart? What nourishes your mind? How are you fulfilled spiritually? To live 'wonder-fully', day by day, it is essential you enjoy a good diet full of the appropriate physical, mental and spiritual foods. Make a meal out of every day! How are you fed, and how do you feed others? Use 10 minutes to list the essential nutrients that sustain and support the real you. Are you eating enough?

What Fills Me with Wonder?

What would you describe as truly inspirational in life? Which people do you revere the most? What subjects fill you with awe, and why? And how often do you allow your inner Self to be inspired? Allot 10 minutes, start wondering and begin to write. The ability to wonder generates boundless energy, excitement and enterprise. Wonder gives flight to the imagination, creativity and new ideas. Above all, wonder inspires the release of potential.

Where Do I Find Peace?

'I take it that what all men are really after is some form or perhaps only some formula of peace,' wrote Joseph Conrad. What are your natural tranquillizers? Where do you find rest? What soothes and heals your stress? How do you help your Self when others have let you down? What do you do right when everything feels wrong? When you feel poor, how do you enrich your Self? List the ways in which you make peace with your Self.

To What Do I Aspire?

'The most important thing is this:' wrote Charles du Bos, 'to be able at any moment to sacrifice what we are for what we could become.' What do you want to make of your life? Whom do you want to become? What do you want to leave behind for those who will follow? Can you list the three main goals that inspire your every action? Right now, off the top of your head, can you describe your primary purpose in life? What, today, do you hope to experience and achieve? Living 'wonder-fully' creates energy, potential and inspiration. Energy needs direction; potential needs purpose; and inspiration needs aspiration.

2
POTENTIAL

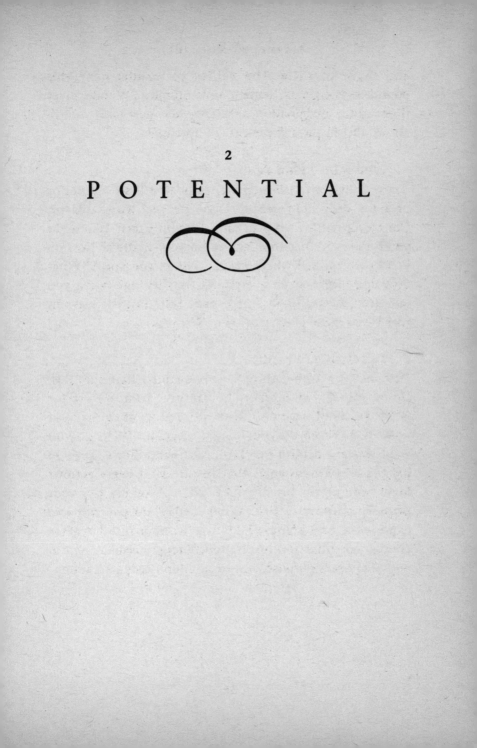

IMAGE

One of the most wonderful things in nature is a glance of the eye; it transcends speech; it is the bodily symbol of identity.

Ralph Waldo Emerson

Your eyes are truly beautiful, intricate miracles of creation. They deliver to you, every waking moment of your life, infinite images of light and shade, colour and radiance.

Through your eyes you can open your true Self to the wonders of the world around you. 'No object is mysterious; the mystery is your eye,' wrote the novelist Elizabeth Bowen.

Each eye is operated by six delicate, strong muscles that work in perfect harmony to grant you the miracle of sight. Your eye muscles perform more than 100,000 movements a day to accommodate a lens that focuses on light rays, an iris that controls the amount of light entering the eye, a retina that receives the focused image, and optic nerves that relay information to the image banks in the brain.

The optic nerves receive information from a mass of light-sensitive cells in the retina called rods and cones. It is estimated that there are 125 million rods and 7 million cones assembled in the retina! The optic nerves somehow collate all of the information from the millions of rods and cones and then transmit the information to the brain at over 250 km an hour. The result is an image so sensitive it may contain as many as 300,000 different distinguishable shades of colour.

Yet sight is much more than a purely physical phenomenon, for it is governed also by the spiritual mechanics of emotion, intellect, intuition and imagination. We see with our eyes, but we also see with our mind, heart and soul—we see with our whole being. In a way, our whole being is like a 'pupil' that is constantly looking and learning. When we see with the whole of our being and not just our eyes, *vision* can become *visionary* and *sight* can be transformed into *insight*.

As well as being able to receive pictures and images from the outside world, we also have an astonishing creative capacity to make our own pictures and images. Each of us is equipped with the emotional–spiritual technology to project, dream, fantasize, visualize and imagine new, fresh and entirely original things. We can paint our own pictures! We can make our own news!

Living 'wonder-fully', at its best, is a wide-eyed adventure in which we purposefully discover and create endless opportunities to see—with our whole being—new scenes, visions and realities that are free to manifest both inside and outside our true Self. *Once we learn how to see again—with our whole being—we are free to see a new present, a new future, and even a new past.*

SELF-IMAGE

See your Self not only with your physical eyes, but with the eyes of your mind, your heart and your soul—see with the whole of your being what a wonder-full potential you are!

You are the living image of your own Self-image. How you choose to *see* your Self greatly influences how you choose to *live* your Self. Health, happiness, love, prosperity and laughter—you can live to see them all if you can perceive that you are entirely deserving, capable and worthy of them all. Alas, the likely alternative is, *if you can't see it happening, you won't live to see it happen*. Such is the enormous power of Self-image.

Self-image is the personal picture each of us carries in the pocket of our hearts. When your Self-image is whole, you feel whole; when your Self-image is in pieces, you may well feel you are falling apart. You are a 'seer', a visionary, and your Self-image is to a large extent a real Self-fulfilling prophecy.

Self-image is a highly creative tool you can use to realize your 'wonder-full' inner potential. Your potential is only as big as it looks. What you see is what there is. What you can perceive is what you can achieve. Thus, if you picture your Self defeated, it is this Self-image alone that is defeating you; picture your Self victorious and your Self-image will ably befriend and assist you.

When we set our sights on a goal, it is, above all else, the quality of our Self-image that determines the quality of our efforts and the quality of the end results. To experience greater happiness, for instance, we must first be willing to see that greater happiness is possible; to enjoy more loving relationships, we must first envision that we are capable of radiating and receiving even more love; and to enjoy greater success, we must first visualize that we are capable of greater success.

To live 'wonder-fully' it is vital to nurture daily a wholesome, ever-evolving Self-image that allows us to see existing possibilities and to create new possibilities for personal growth, inner development and Self-fulfilment. An expansive Self-image is a key part of your personal miracle kit; it can equip you with the necessary belief, esteem and insight to help manifest your visions and your dreams. Perhaps the best Self-image of all is to visualize your Self as a spark of the universal, creative Intelligence. Make a commitment to set aside a day to experiment seeing your Self as the custodian of a universal, creative potential and I believe all your feelings, actions, interactions and experiences will be highly enriched and rewarding. *It all depends on how you see it!* Change your old Self-image and in time you will discover a new Self-fulfilment.

MIRRORS

The world is a mirror, and you are my reflection. If I am different to you, you will be different to me.

To see only with the physical eye creates a visual illusion in which the world around us stands separate and apart from us. When we allow our true Self to look with the inner eye of the heart, mind and soul, we discover something quite different: we see, in truth, we are part of a whole—and we just can't help being wholly connected to everything and everybody!

This holistic, poetic intuition is also the new view of modern science, which now sees that we live in a participatory universe in which observer and observed are inseparable. Erwin Schrodinger, the Austrian physicist who won the Nobel Prize for Physics in 1933, saw that, 'Subject and object are but one. The barrier between them cannot be said to have broken down as a result of recent experience in the physical world, for this barrier *does not exist.*'

Werner Heisenberg, the German physicist who won the Nobel Prize for Physics in 1932, also reached a similar conclusion: 'The common division of the world into subject and object, inner world and outer world, body and soul is no longer adequate.' Science and intuition are in agreement, then, that our relationship with the 'outside' world is a lot more intimate than appears when we look only through our physical eyes.

The psychology of Self-image suggests that, in truth, how we choose to picture our Self helps to paint the world we see around us. Seeing is the cause; experience is the effect. Thus, if we change the way we see the world, we may well change the way we experience it. The participatory universe theory of quantum physics agrees that the way in which we observe the world may in a fundamental way shape the world.

Ultimately, then, the world around us mirrors the world within us, and vice versa. The people we meet are reflections of who we are, for they too are our mirrors. Their attitudes and behaviours, their strengths and their weaknesses are, in truth, our own. Don't try, therefore, to change the world around you; change your Self and the world will follow.

INSIGHTS

To see things as they are, the eyes must be open; to see
things as other than they are, they must open even wider; to
see things as better than they are, they must be open to
the full.

Antonio Machado

To be truly happy and fulfilled it is vital we turn our gaze
inward where we can learn how to see again with the
whole of our being. In my *Living Wonder-fully* workshops,
participants create time and space to reflect and gain
insight about the physical, emotional and spiritual
mechanics of sight. When it comes to happiness and
fulfilment, so much depends on how you see your Self and
on how you see *your* world. The following seven *insights*
may well help you to live more 'wonder-fully'.

1. *You make your Self in your own Self-image.*
   Self-image is an inner creative force that can shape and
   alter character, personality and behaviour. Every
   thought and feeling, every action is entirely faithful to
   your own Self-image. Transform your Self-image and
   you will transform who you are.
2. *The eye 'receives' what the mind 'perceives'.*
   Eyesight is more than a physical 'peep show'; it is a
   whole-being event in which we see with our mind, our
   heart and our soul. 'Eyes will not see when the heart
   wishes them to be blind,' wrote Seneca. 'The eye obeys
   exactly the action of the mind,' wrote Emerson. Your
   eyes will select only what you are prepared to see.
3. *'We see things not as they are, but as we are,' wrote*
   Immanuel Kant.
   The Yogis illustrate this truth by saying, 'when a

44

pickpocket meets a saint, he only sees his pockets!'
Change your mind and you will change what you see.
'Human thought, like God, makes the world in its own
image,' wrote Adam Clayton.

4. *Whatever your mind looks at magnifies!*
   The more you look, the more there is to see. If you
   focus only on your burdens, more burdens will appear
   to you. Alternatively, if you are willing to look for
   blessings, you will soon discover more blessings than
   you could ever imagine. Become 'good looking'—look
   for the good and the good will appear! Whatever you
   focus on, flourishes!

5. *Be careful what you look for, you will find it.*
   Your eyes will always find what you are looking for. A
   cynic sees despair before hope, a hypochondriac sees
   illness before health. You can choose what you want to
   see and, consequently, how you want to live. If you are
   willing to look afresh, you can begin to live afresh.

6. *There is always another way of looking at things.*
   We blink on average 25 times a minute; we have,
   therefore, 25 possibilities a minute to see things
   differently. Never, ever is there only one way to see
   something. A different outlook inspires a different
   outcome. Change the perception and you can change
   the experience. 'The Eye altering alters all,' wrote the
   visionary poet William Blake.

7. *You will see a difference if you are prepared to see things
   differently.*
   Just because you can't see something doesn't mean you
   shouldn't look for it. Adjust your focus, alter your
   sights and re-view your Self. If you will only start
   looking, things can then begin to appear. *The eyes
   have it!*

RE-VISION

As a man sees, so he is; as a man is, so he sees.

The good news is that you are free to transform your life at any waking moment—if, that is, you are prepared first to transform your Self-image. Review, revise and re-dedicate! First, *review* who you are; second, *revise* what you want and who you want to be; third, set your sights again and *re-dedicate* your Self. A new you can evolve if you are willing to see your Self anew. As long as you hold on to your vision, your vision has a chance to come true. Everything begins with a vision.

The following three exercises are creative growth games that use image and imagination to help you realize your abundant, 'wonder-full' potential. 'The Possible's slow fuse is lit/by the Imagination,' wrote the American poet, Emily Dickinson.

Image Analysis:

How do you see your Self? Can you see how good it is to be you? If you were to draw your potential what sort of picture would it make? Set aside an hour of your life to create a personal inventory in which you record:

'One of the strengths I see in my Self is...'
(List 10 strengths)
'One of the skills I see in my Self is...'
(List 10 skills)
'One of the lovable qualities I see in my Self is...'
(List 10 lovable qualities)

'One of the best things I can see I have achieved in my life is...'
(List 10 achievements)
'One of the things I look forward to seeing my Self achieve or experience in my life is...'
(List 10 visions)

This could be the shortest or longest hour of your life! Whatever happens, it will certainly be an eye-opener! This conscious Self-exploration and Self-discovery will provide the information and Self-knowledge on which to build a Self-image, Self-esteem and Self-worth. You are worth what you can see.

Image Rehearsal

How would you like to be different? What would you like to do differently?

Perhaps you would like to be more confident or warm, or to smile more. Using a creative technique called *Image Rehearsal* you can use the imagination to develop and evolve your inner Self. Seeing a difference can actually make a difference.

If you want, for instance, to smile more, you can use the following *Image Rehearsal* twice a day (first thing in the morning and last thing at night). In between these times, act on it!:

1. Allow your Self to relax and to breathe fully and freely.
2. Breathe in, repeating on the in-breath, 'I would like to smile more;' on the out-breath picture your Self smiling freely without fear or inhibition. Smile as you breathe out. Repeat this five times.

3. Breathe in and repeat, 'I can see my Self smiling more;' on the out-breath continue to imagine your Self smiling easily. Smile as you breathe out. Repeat five times.

4. Breathe in and repeat, 'I can see that it is OK to smile more;' on the out-breath continue to see your Self smiling effortlessly. Smile as you breathe out. Repeat five times.

5. Breathe in and repeat, 'I can see I can smile more;' on the out-breathe enjoy seeing your Self smiling naturally. Smile as you breathe out. Repeat five times.

The more you imagine something, the more real it feels. Imagination is a creative tool that can inspire wonder-full results. You can use positive mental pictures to affirm, to create and to realize what you want to see happen in your life. *Image rehearsal* works if you are willing.

Image Projection

What sort of person would you like to see your Self become? Paint a picture—using either paints, prose, poetry or flow diagrams—of how you would like to see your Self in three months' time. What key events, experiences or achievements would you like to see your Self manifest?

Consider 1) your health and fitness; 2) your relationships with family, friends and partner; 3) your finances; 4) your growth and education; 5) your time for fun; 6) your spiritual inspiration. Set your sights on a goal, clarify your thoughts, focus your actions and see the goal getting nearer every day until it has been achieved (see

Part IV: 'Purpose').

Visualization is a vital key to successful goal-setting: if you can't realistically see your Self doing something you won't ever see your Self do it. You can create *Self Projection* charts for five years ahead, one year ahead, one month ahead, one week ahead. Each and every day do your personal best, and know too that, ultimately, *life knows best*. Let your imagination run free!

THOUGHT

What a wonder-full thing a thought is. Everything comes from a thought; a thought gives birth to everything.

Michael Furber

There is a fantastic force in life that has an almost magical power to transform fatigue into energy, despair into delight and anxiety into action. This force can make 'bad' things 'good' and 'wrong' things 'right'. An 'upset' can become a 'set-up', a 'misfortune' can become a 'favour' and a 'failure' can become a 'success'. This magical force has the power to decide.

The great news is that you are perfectly entitled to use this fantastic force, if you so choose. If you do, you may well find, quite miraculously, that obstacles can turn into opportunities, adversity into advantage, breakdowns into breakthroughs and unhappy endings into bright new beginnings. This force, if you haven't already guessed, is the power of thought.

Thought is creative: the way you think is the way it is. For instance, if you choose to think rain makes you miserable, you will probably be miserable each time it rains; if you *know* you fail at interviews, you will probably fail your next interview; if you choose to believe you can't make friends easily, you will probably find it very difficult meeting new people. A different way of thinking can make all the difference.

ATTITUDE

Our life is what our thoughts make it.

Marcus Aurelius

Be careful what you choose to think, for you will never go higher than your thoughts. There is no such thing as an idle thought or a wasted word. Every thought you entertain leaves a mark, imparts an influence and casts a consequence. Indeed, I would go as far as to say that *the quality of your thoughts determines the quality of your life*. Think well, live well.

A healthy attitude cannot, on its own, guarantee an endless garland of rosy outcomes. For instance, choosing to think you *won't* fail an interview does not automatically mean you *can't* fail it. A healthy attitude can, however, inspire and supply the necessary energy, belief, action, initiative and creative endeavour that insures you bring out the best in your Self, whatever the outcome.

A week or two after I set up my very first NHS Stress Buster Clinic, a young gentleman by the name of Philip came to visit. Poorly dressed, unshaven and exhausted, he delivered a long monologue on the evils of unemployment and how being out of work was 'driving him out of his head'. He told me he thought it was impossible to find work—so impossible he had given up looking! Like our friend who wanted to win the pools without entering, Philip's thoughts had rendered a Self-fulfilling prophecy!

When I eventually asked Philip how he benefited from

being unemployed, he almost hit the roof! I explained, tactfully, that Philip's destructive, non-helpful way of thinking was making a 'bad' situation worse. In fact, I went further. I even that being unemployed was not intrinsically 'bad' or 'good'—*nothing is intrinsically 'bad' or 'good'; 'bad' and 'good' are what we make them!* Philip left our first meeting with a lot to think about.

When I saw Philip next, about three weeks later, I did not recognize him. He was still unemployed, but he was sprightly, less dejected and, above all, hopeful. 'Something clicked,' he said, 'I'm looking for work again.' The joy on his face as he spoke about watching his children grow was a delight to see. Philip was benefiting from his unemployment, and others were benefiting too, including the community centre for the elderly where he had enrolled as a volunteer.

Your attitude is your Aladdin's lamp—an open, creative frame of mind will always make a magic that is different to the magic a closed, destructive mind will make. Whatever happens, you can always make the most of a situation if you are prepared to make the most of your thinking. It's not what happens to you that makes life 'good' or 'bad'; *it's what you do with what happens to you* that really counts. Change your mind and you can change your life.

'ESTATE OF MIND'

As a man thinketh so is he, and as a man chooseth so is he.

Ralph Waldo Emerson

We build our own fortunes—and most of these fortunes accumulate from a healthy 'estate of mind'. Everything is ultimately an attitude. Life is an attitude. For instance, if you are happy, it is because you think and feel you are happy. 'I am happy and content because I think I am,' wrote Alain René Lessage. If you are sad, it is because you think and feel you are sad. 'Nothing is miserable unless you think it so,' wrote Boethius. You have the casting vote—always, anytime, right now.

Do you choose to be open-minded or do you choose to be closed-minded? Do you choose to think differently or do you choose to think the same? Do you choose to be optimistic or do you choose to be pessimistic? Thinking is not an involuntary act beyond your control; it is an act of personal choice. You can choose how you think—you can choose the direction of your thoughts, their frequency, intensity and the subject of your thoughts.

People can *help* you to have happy thoughts, but nobody can *make* you happy. That is your choice. Similarly, a flat tyre in a country lane on a wet Sunday may well *encourage* you to have miserable thoughts, but a flat tyre cannot actually *make* you miserable. Physically, rationally, there is no way a flat tyre can make you have a headache; unless, that is, the tyre actually bounces on your head! You think for your Self and, ultimately, it is you who makes up your mind whether or not a flat tyre is a mere inconvenience or an international incident.

Sometimes we are so close to our thoughts we actually

forget that we create them. You are shaped by your thoughts, but you are not, actually, your thoughts. Thoughts are tools; every time you choose to remind your Self that you are more than your thoughts and that you can choose how to think, you are taking a massive step towards your own personal freedom and fulfilment.

MINDFULNESS

The mind is its own place, and in itself
Can make a heaven of hell, a hell of heaven.

Milton

When I one day become Minister of Education (in my dreams!) the very first thing I want to do is to introduce an 'Art of Thinking' module to the national syllabus. Thought is a vital tool, and thinking an essential skill. How can any of us begin to fulfil our Self if we have only a partial understanding and control of our minds?

By being mindful, observant and consciously aware of how we think we can begin to exercise our power of control. Ultimately, each of us decides whether or not we choose either to relinquish control of our thoughts and leave everything to *chance* or to grasp the reins of our thoughts and make everything a *choice*. Growth is an offshoot of choice.

Nine Thoughts about Thought

1. *You are the originator of your thoughts.* You think for your Self and you choose for your Self. Anyone can influence, encourage and prompt you, but no one can make you think a certain way—unless, that is, you allow this. Exercise your power of choice.

54

2. *Thoughts are governed by the law of cause and effect.* Hope inspires a different effect to despair; Self-belief inspires a different effect to Self-doubt; forgiveness inspires a different effect to resentment; and love inspires a different effect to hate. A different outlook *effects* a different outcome.

3. *Thoughts are also governed by the law of like attracts like.* The more pessimistic you are, the easier it is to be pessimistic; the more optimistic you are, the easier it is to be optimistic. Pessimism attracts doubt, mistrust, fear and anxiety; optimism attracts belief, hope, joy and action. Repeating a thought has an accumulative effect.

4. *You are the product of your thoughts,* yet you are not your thoughts. 'What a person thinks about all day long, they become,' wrote Emerson. I think, therefore I am; I think, therefore I become. Thinking, like Self-image, is a Self-fulfilling prophecy. Improve your thinking and you will see improvements in your Self.

5. *Thought is creative.* 'It is the disposition of the thought that altereth the nature of the thing,' wrote John Lyly. Courageous thinking creates a different reality than fearful thinking does; warm, cheerful thoughts create a different reality than do cold, cheerless thoughts. Alter your context and you alter the consequences. Happiness is only ever a thought away.

6. *The way you think about your Self determines the way you see your Self,* and vice versa. Change what you think and what you see will change also.

7. *A thought about someone else is a thought about you.* Whatever you think about someone, the effects of those thoughts register on your body and your mind. Hating someone hurts your nerves, your muscles, your

heart and your mind. The price of hating another is loving your Self less. Thoughts rebound. Take time to contemplate the far-reaching implications of this.

8. *Thought is suggestive.* Behind every word and every thought there is an underlying, active 'power of suggestion' which affirms and makes it so. A train of thought puts a proposal into motion: keep the thought and your proposal will manifest and become real. A hypochondriac illustrates this point perfectly.

9. *What you think becomes your goal.* The brain takes everything for real—to the brain there is no such thing as conjecture, opinion, idle thought, imagination, or 'I didn't really mean that.' Thus, if you programme 'I can't' into your brain often enough, your brain will automatically set about harnessing all of its resources to process and 'make real' your thought. What you think about is what your brain strives for.

HEALTH

Disease is an experience of mortal mind. It is fear made manifest on the body.

Mary Baker Eddy

A single thought can have a profound, multiplying effect on the entire chemistry of your brain and body, altering breath, circulation and blood flow, activating or soothing your nerves, increasing or reducing muscle tension, speeding up or slowing down heartbeat, raising or lowering blood-pressure, dispensing or withholding vital hormones and enhancing or exhausting the immune system.

Thoughts can either be medicines or poisons, depending on their quality and type. Every thought is, in effect, a prescription for harmony or disharmony, ease or dis-ease, health or illness. The harmony of your mind supports the harmony of your body and vice versa. Mind and body are inseparable, integrated parts of a single whole. Thus, the quality of your thinking helps to determine the quality of your physical, mental, emotional and spiritual health.

When I first began my NHS *Relaxation for Positive Change* Clinic, I had the pleasure of meeting a woman called Sharma who described her Self as 'stiff as a board' and 'worried sick'. Sharma was in physical knots all over her body; she experienced, in particular, shooting pains all the way up her neck. Her neck pains restricted her movements and as a result she was only able to see straight ahead; seeing side-to-side was too painful.

Sharma was physically tense because she was emotionally tense. The tension was the result of a fraught relationship with her boss at work whom she had allowed to exploit her. 'I have worked in a factory for 12 years and I hate my job,' she told me, 'He [the boss] is a real pain in the neck!' Sharma often called her boss a 'pain in the neck'. When I first pointed out the connection between her neck pains and her favourite saying, Sharma laughed and laughed. Sharma had stayed in the job for 12 years because she could see no way out. Like her neck, her thoughts were not able to see from side to side. With relaxation, Sharma changed her thoughts—and her job!

Everything is interconnected; everything is interwoven. Physical indigestion may be caused by a reluctance to accept and 'digest' a life event, such as moving house; a stomach ulcer may be exacerbated by a thought or an idea that is 'hard to stomach'; a poor breathing pattern may be induced by too much stress and not enough 'breathing space'; and a dis-eased heart may really be an issue of love and acceptance. The whole answer rests with the whole person.

Many of the most ancient and well-established healing traditions have evolved from knowledge of the mind–body–spirit connection. Meditation, hypnotherapy, auto-suggestion, massage, reflexology, acupuncture and yoga, for instance, recognize that health and fulfilment are products of a balanced body and balanced mind working in harmony.

Modern medical research is at last rediscovering the importance of providing 'the full treatment' to the 'full person' for ensuring the 'fullness of health'. Psychosomatic medicine (mind and body), bio-psycho-social medicine (body, mind and society) and psycho-neuro-immunology (mind, brain and immune system) are all recent trends in orthodox medicine that support the notion that *to live healthily you must think healthily*.

AFFIRMATION

Man's attitude to life, determines his destiny.
                                            Albert Schweitzer

If you can raise the quality of your thoughts, you can raise the quality of your health and the quality of your life. One very simple, effective way of doing this is to harness the 'suggestion power' or 'programming power' of your thoughts by practising affirmations. A daily routine of well-chosen affirmations can assert a real, tangible difference in your life.

Everything you think is an affirmation. If you think, 'I'm lovable' your mind, brain and body affirms it; if you think, 'I hate my Self' your mind, brain and body affirms it. Everything you think is digested, assimilated and acted upon. The laws of cause and effect and like attract like, mentioned earlier, work on your affirmations to produce a response that is always parallel and equal. Your whole being aims, always, to support, realize and manifest whatever you think. Remember: *thought is creative.*

So-called 'negative affirmations' often proliferate when we least need them, such as during times of stress, illness and disappointment. At the onset of a cold we pronounce, 'I feel terrible,' 'I'm getting a cold' and 'I'm all bunged up'. These are verbal commands—keep in mind, *whatever you think about becomes your goal.* When our friends hear we have a cold, they phone us to commiserate: 'It must be awful,' they affirm. 'Yes it is,' we affirm! 'How do you feel?' they ask. 'Awful,' we affirm. 'Describe the symptoms' they say. And we do!

Affirmations can come from any direction. Commiseration and sympathy from others, for example, can be a type of affirmation that supports you *in* your predicament rather than supporting you *out* of it. When you read in the paper next day, 'Flu Epidemic Hits Town,' watch how you behave! I firmly believe that most flu epidemics 'recruit' 30 per cent more people as a result of the enormously influential affirmations pumped out by the mass media.

Thinking is a precursor to feeling and experience. Therefore, while you should always be careful not to suppress anything, you should also be mindful of the temptation to use words, thoughts, feelings and *behaviours* that may well be affirming illness and thereby hindering the healing and recovery process. You will face a similar challenge also during times of stress, apparent failure, disappointment and hardship—be careful, always, of what you are affirming: what you affirm is what you encourage to happen.

Perhaps the most popular example of a verbal affirmation for better health is the one devised by the French psychotherapist Emile Coue, who in the 1920s prescribed to his clients, 'Every day in every way I am getting better and better.' Behavioural psychologists also use similar 'reinforcement' techniques to encourage clients to reduce anxiety and heal phobias. Affirmations work.

Creating 'Wonder-full' Affirmations

1. *Remember, everything is an affirmation.* What you say, think, feel and do affirms and encourages an effect that must happen. You are always sowing seeds: plant flowers, not weeds!

2. *The more relaxed you are, the more suggestible you are.* As you unwind, you enter a realm of relaxed reception where your unconscious mind can more fully embrace, accept and integrate new ideas. Thus, it is good to begin a sequence of affirmations with a short period of relaxed breathing.

3. *The more you repeat an affirmation, the stronger it becomes.* The more you use affirmations consciously the more useful they will become to you.

4. *The more you concentrate, the more concentrated your affirmation becomes.* By being focused, single-minded and attentive, the influence of your affirmations can expand and grow. Be aware that *whatever your mind holds on to, heightens.*

5. *The more dynamic and enthusiastic you are, the more power your affirmations will generate.* The more energy you use, the more energized your affirmations will

become. The more enthusiastically you work at affirmations the more enthusiastically affirmations will work for you. Be joyful.

6. *Say it and see it.* The left side of your brain thinks with words; the right side of your brain thinks with pictures. The most powerful affirmations of all, therefore, are affirmations that combine imagery and word play.

7. *Behave as if you believe it.* Behave as if you are already starting to achieve what you are aiming for. Affirmations work best when what you say and what you see are supported by what you do. Behaviour is the finishing touch.

8. *Make your affirmations active and progressive.* Saying 'I want to get better' is unhelpful because the affirmation contains no thought, image or suggestion that you *are* getting better. Replace 'I want' with 'I can', 'I am becoming', 'I am gaining', 'I am achieving' or 'I am developing', for example.

9. *Don't lie.* If your confidence is currently collapsed I would advise you not to begin with, 'I am great today;' if your foot is in plaster I would not advise starting with, 'I am healed!' Use suggestion, encouragement and reassurance, not lies.

10. *Be positive.* In my experience an affirmation like, 'I am becoming less stressed,' does not work as well as 'I am becoming more relaxed.' The 'I'm not going to...' affirmations create resistance. Try saying to your Self, for instance, 'I'm not going to think of a pink elephant.' My bet is that you have just thought of a pink elephant—I also bet that more pink elephants will pop into your head again before the day is out! Affirm the positive.

11. *Feel it!* Feelings resonate throughout the whole of your being, so it is good to feel what you affirm. Every affirmation will create a physical sensation somewhere in the body. An affirmation such as, 'I can love my Self more' may well create a physical sensation in the heart. Feel your affirmations physically, mentally and emotionally. Breathe in to where the feeling is. Can you associate a smell, taste, touch or sound with your affirmation? Whatever you affirm, feel it and be it.

12. *Make your periods of repetition regular, routine and frequent.* It is more beneficial to perform several short periods of affirmation at regular times in the day than to complete one long period at irregular times. With a regular routine you may soon find that your unconscious mind begins to recite your affirmations automatically at the given times.

13. *Practise your affirmations three times a day to begin with:* first thing in the morning, once during the day and last thing at night is absolutely ideal. A morning routine helps you to begin the day as you mean to end it; once during the day acts as a timely reminder; and last thing at night encourages the unconscious to continue repeating the affirmation for as long as you sleep—you can then claim you are performing eight hours of affirmation a day!

14. *Make a 21-day contract with your Self.* The great news is that a lifetime of awful affirmations does not require another lifetime of helpful affirmations to reverse the damage! In fact, 21 days—less than a single month—is all you need. Isn't that wonder-full?!

The following sequence of 'I choose' affirmations are designed to remind you that you have a choice about what you think, and that ultimately *life is a series of choices.* Whether or not you choose to experiment with these affirmations, or make time to create your own, is also your choice! We are blessed with choice, for by exercising our power of choice we can actually determine how we live.

Begin by developing a deep, long, slow breathing pattern in which you allow the breath to breathe you. Breathe freely without pause, allowing the inhalation to flow into an exhalation easily, effortlessly and naturally. Consciously allow your Self, physically, mentally and emotionally, to let go of everything and hold on to nothing. Relax. When you are suitably poised, begin:

Breathe in: *Affirm: 'I choose to be alive, happy and well.'*
Breathe out: *Picture your Self alive, happy and well, and feel it.*
              (Repeat three times)

Breathe in: *Affirm: 'I choose to live creatively, with wonder.'*
Breathe out: *Picture what you say, and feel it.*
              (Repeat three times)

Breathe in: *Affirm: 'I choose to radiate and receive love.'*
Breathe out: *Picture what you say, and feel it.*
              (Repeat three times)

Breathe in: *Affirm: 'I choose to radiate and receive joy.'*
Breathe out: *Picture what you say, and feel it.*
              (Repeat three times)

Breathe in: *Affirm: 'I choose to radiate and receive laughter.'*
Breathe out: *Picture what you say, and feel it.*
(Repeat three times)

Breathe in: *Affirm: 'I choose to radiate and receive truth.'*
Breathe out: *Picture what you say, and feel it.*
(Repeat three times)

Breathe in: *Affirm: 'I choose to radiate and receive peace.'*
Breathe out: *Picture what you say, and feel it.*
(Repeat three times)

Breathe in: *Affirm: 'I choose to radiate and receive prosperity.'*
Breathe out: *Picture what you say, and feel it.*
(Repeat three times)

Breathe in: *Affirm: 'I choose to learn from every experience in life.'*
Breathe out: *Picture what you say, and feel it.*
(Repeat three times)

Breathe in: *Affirm: 'I choose to benefit from every experience in life.'*
Breathe out: *Picture what you say, and feel it.*
(Repeat three times)

Breathe in: *Affirm: 'I choose to prosper from every experience in life.'*

Breathe out: *Picture what you say, and feel it.*
(Repeat three times)

Breathe in: *Affirm: 'I choose to prosper from every experience in life.'*

Breathe out: *Picture what you say, and feel it.*
(Repeat three times)

Breathe in: *Affirm: 'I choose to grow with every experience in life.'*

Breathe out: *Picture what you say, and feel it.*
(Repeat three times)

BELIEF

Man is What he Believes

Anton Chekhov

Michael, a physician, had suffered from intermittent bouts of insomnia for as long as he could remember. When he came to see me at my *Feel Great, Meditate Clinic*, he told me he had not slept a wink for the last five nights. He was tired, gaunt and ready to try anything that might help. Together we created over the space of an hour or so a programme of meditation, relaxation and lifestyle enhancement.

Michael is one of these enlightened doctors who only takes or prescribes medication as a last resort. That night, however, he reluctantly decided he had to take just one tablet as he needed all the rest he could get to help to prepare him for a very important presentation the following day. So he got into bed, turned off the light, and reached for the tablet sitting on the bedside cabinet.

Before he knew it, it was morning. He had slept the whole night through! The natural light of the sun's rays came pouring through the bedroom window and, as he threw back the bedsheets, Michael saw to his great surprise that the sleeping tablet was still there on the bedside cabinet. What had happened? The tablet was indeed untouched—but Michael's loose pyjama button was now missing!

There is no scientific evidence that I have ever read that suggests loose pajama buttons can help cure insomnia! However, because Michael *believed* he was swallowing a tablet, his mind, brain and body 'swallowed' the idea also and then responded appropriately. The medical profession would happily accept this story as a normal everyday healing by *placebo*. The word 'placebo' is translated as, *pleasing belief.*

The placebo effect is one of the most convincing demonstrations of the medicinal power of mind over matter, or, *belief over body.* Placebo medications containing non-medicinal substances such as chalk have been used to successfully treat headaches, migraines, high blood-pressure, travel sickness, asthma and, of course, insomnia. Such is the power of belief.

FAITH

And how can I believe in God when just last week, I got my tongue caught in the roller of an electric typewriter?
Woody Allen

You have, like everybody else, developed throughout your life a faith, or belief system, which helps and serves you to understand and make sense of your inner Self and of the world around you. For as long as you live, your thoughts, feelings, perceptions and actions will be entirely faithful to this personal belief system of yours. Your belief system sets the boundaries of what is and what is not possible, probable or passable for you in your life. *What you believe will be how you live.*

If you do not believe that you deserve to enjoy a happy, fulfilling relationship, you will not allow your Self to enjoy one. If you doubt that you are entitled to greater success in life, you will not allow your Self to be more successful. If you mistrust that you are entitled to earn as much money as you like, your money supply will always be limited. If you cannot believe you can begin again, your fresh start will go stale on you. What you work out in your mind tends to work out in your life.

Angela was my very first client when I began my own private practice in psychotherapy. Tall and very much overweight, Angela was one of the most imposing characters I have ever met. I initially offered her tea; she replied, 'Let's not waste time.' After she had told me I looked too young to be of any use, she came straight to the point: 'The new man in my life is far too nice, ' she said. I was immediately at a loss, for nowhere in my psychology textbooks was there a listing for 'The Too Nice Man in Your Life'!

When Angela said 'too nice' I thought, at first, that she meant he squeezed the toothpaste for her, blew her nose for her and basically never left her alone. On the contrary, this man gave Angela all the space she required. He treated Angela with respect, courtesy and an open honesty she had never experienced before. She had a say in everything: for the first time in her life she was allowed to decide whether or not to make love at night. Angela was at last an equal: she told her Self she should be happy, yet she had never felt so miserable.

Angela's pain was being caused because two of her

major belief statements were currently being disproved. Angela had previously believed, as a result of a string of deceitful, manipulative relationships, that men only caused pain and that she was 'not good enough'. The new man in her life was now disproving these beliefs. I explained to Angela that until she updated her belief system she would not allow her true Self to enjoy, accept or deserve her new relationship. Sadly, Angela held on to her old beliefs and let go of her new man. I think of her often, and I wish her well.

Most of our belief systems are completely outdated. To begin with, we inherit our parents' belief systems. What we first believe about love, friendship, happiness, success and life in general we learn from observing how our parents live. 'The oven is hot,' we are warned; we then go ahead and burn our Self anyway and so we believe that our mum and dad know best. As children we soon learn to believe that everything our parents tell us is the truth.

From conception we begin to create a mental–emotional reference guide called 'Life: How to Survive it' which is based primarily on the beliefs our parents act out. Harmful belief systems evolve when, for instance, a child witnesses parents fighting again and again and notes 'love hurts', or when a child is always told there will be tears before bedtime and he or she equates this with, 'happiness does not last', or when parents tell a child continually that he or she is bad, silly or naughty and the child learns, 'I hate my Self' and 'I am not good enough.'

Most of these beliefs—and a few new ones, too—will also be endorsed by teachers, friends, work colleagues, the boss and our own personal experience. You initially created a belief system that, like the child your were, was flexible and adjustable; unfortunately, over time, if we are not vigilant the belief system can, like an old gramophone needle, begin to stick, stop and stay where it is. Unless we change the needle and change our beliefs we may never play a new tune again.

If like most adults your belief system is at least 20 years out of date, it may no longer be helping, protecting and enlightening you, as was its initial purpose. It may be hindering, arresting and imprisoning you. Instead of living in the present you may well be replaying the patterns of the past over and over again. If so, seemingly fresh new beginnings will lead inevitably to familiar old endings. *To change what is to be, you must change what it is you believe.*

VALUE

Belief consists in accepting the affirmations of the soul; unbelief in denying them.

Ralph Waldo Emerson

Your belief system sets the boundaries of what is to be and what is not to be. You can only ever be as big as your belief system; you can only be as wealthy as your Self-worth; and you can only ever be as valuable as your Self-value. Thus, the more you believe in your true Self, the more you can be; the more you value your Self, the more valuable you can become.

Who you believe you are determines who you are and who you will become. 'If thou believest thou art a body, thou art divided from the universe. If thou believest thou art a spirit, thou art a spark of the eternal fire. If thou believest thou art the divine self, thou art all things,' wrote the Yogi, Vivekananda. The more you believe in your Self, the more there is to believe in.

We can sometimes go beyond our belief system when, for example, we experience a 'wonder-full', unexpected moment of love, success, fortune or happiness. We have the capacity to surprise our Self and to surpass our Self. I am an amateur golfer—very amateur! Golf really is a long walk with lots of little disappointments! During an average round of golf I can play a wide range of shots—this is a flattering description of what I do, which is hit the ball all over the place. However, I can occasionally surprise and surpass my Self by playing a world-class golf shot.

Whenever we surprise and surpass our belief system we must choose either to *alter or falter*. We will falter if we stick to the Self-limiting affirmations that usually proliferate after a surprise, such as, 'It was luck,' 'Wait 'til next time,' 'Unbelievable,' 'Incredible,' 'This is too good to be true' and 'It won't happen again.' If, however, we choose to alter our belief system we can accept life's surprises and even attract greater ones. Please remember this: *you will only be served what you feel you deserve.*

TRUST

Self-trust is the essence of heroism.

Ralph Waldo Emerson

The word 'believe' is derived from the Old English *belyfan*, which means 'to have faith', 'to love' and 'to trust'. Learning to trust that you can be more than you are and that you can do more than you do is essential to living 'wonder-fully'. The following six guidelines may be of help.

1. *We live in a land of make believe.* We are all of us built
   by belief. You are the personification of your belief
   system. As you evolve and experiment with your belief
   system you can alter and transform your Self. Change
   one personal belief about your Self today, and watch
   your Self change. 'If thou canst believe, all things *are*
   possible to him that believeth,' (Mark 9:23).

2. *What you believe will be how you live.* You are entirely
   faithful to your conscious and unconscious beliefs. The
   power of belief motivates, energizes and propels your
   every thought and action. You live your convictions.
   You will gain if you believe you can succeed; you will
   lose if you believe you will fail. In the Hindu holy
   book, the *Bhagavad Gita*, it is written, 'A man consists
   of the faith that is in him. What his faith is, he is.'

3. *What you believe is what you perceive.* You can only ever
   perceive what you believe. Change what you believe
   and you will change what you see. Believe in and look
   for the 'good' in a 'bad' situation and, by magic, the
   'good' will manifest. St Augustine wrote, 'Faith is to
   believe what you do not yet see; the reward for this
   faith is to see what you believe.'

4. *What you believe is what you conceive.* Your thoughts can
   only ever be as beautiful as your beliefs. If you liberate
   your beliefs you can liberate your thoughts—then you
   are free to fulfil your Self. 'Under all that we think,
   lives all we believe, like the ultimate veil of our spirits,'
   wrote Antonio Machado.

5. *What you believe will be what you achieve.* Consciously
   and unconsciously you must believe in your Self if you
   are to achieve for your Self the victories of love,
   happiness, peace and fulfilment. *To believe or not to*

believe, that is the question! Belief upholds the possible; doubt tears it down. 'According to your faith be it unto you,' (Matthew 9:29).

6. *What you believe to be true, is your truth.* Your reality is fashioned not only by how you see your Self and how you think but by what you believe. Albert Ellis's marvellous *ABC* model illustrates this point perfectly. 'A' stands for activating event; 'B' stands for belief; 'C' stands for consequence. Whatever you believe about 'A' will determine 'C'. Thus, if you believe failures are only harmful you may well fall; if, however, you believe failures can be instructive and helpful you may well rise.

ASSERTION

It is not just as we take it,
This mystical world of ours,
Life's field will yield as we make it
A harvest of thorns or of flowers.

Johann von Goethe

Throughout your life you carve (consciously and unconsciously) your own personal philosophy which you then uphold and develop with every image, thought, belief and action. We are all of us philosophers for we all of us have developed a belief system which we follow and adhere to. We are disciples of our own personal doctrine or creed. What you believe is your greatest inspiration.

Because you are, ultimately, more than your beliefs, you are free at any time in your life to assert a new idea, a new thought, a new belief. 'The Belief Licence' is a personal creative growth game that grants you greater licence to assert your beliefs and intent on a daily basis. Using the power of affirmation, you recite, visualize, feel and ultimately affirm and endorse your chosen beliefs.

'The Belief Licence' below is an example of the kind of personal statements you might want to endorse. Each theme is written according to the guidelines given for affirmations on page 60. Begin and end with relaxation. As you breathe in, recite a belief; as you breathe out, visualize and feel the effect. And remember: the best affirmation of all is to behave as if you already believe in them all. Whatever themes you want to assert, the following may act as a useful guideline:

- 'I believe in ever-evolving love. I am on Earth to learn how to love. I deserve ever-evolving love.'
- 'I believe in ever-embracing joy. I can radiate and receive more joy. I deserve ever-embracing joy.'
- 'I believe in ever-beautiful laughter. Happiness is a way of travelling. I deserve ever-beautiful laughter.'
- 'I believe in ever-enlightening truth. To mine own Self I shall be true. I deserve ever-enlightening truth.'
- 'I believe in ever-expanding peace. I can find my peace of mind. I deserve ever-expanding peace.'
- 'I believe in ever-increasing integrity. I can integrate everything with peace. I deserve ever-increasing integrity.'
- 'I believe in ever-enriching success. I can be even more successful. I deserve ever-enriching success.'
- 'I believe in ever-fulfilling freedom. I can set my Self free. I deserve ever-fulfilling freedom.'

WORDS

> How wonderful is the human voice! It is indeed the organ of the soul.
>
> *Henry Wadsworth Longfellow*

Words are wonder-full! Every word you send out into the world casts a consequence, conjures up a return and weaves an effect that inevitably shapes and alters your life. You really do get to 'keep your word' in life! Your word is your bond, and you have the 'say-so' to choose how you will live and how things will be.

Like thoughts and beliefs, words have enough magic to create a massive change in the chemistry of your body. Muscles, nerves, heart rate, lungs and blood-pressure react to the words you and other people say. A happy compliment, for instance, is (I believe) nutritionally equivalent to at least a week's supply of healthy, organic fruit and vegetables; a criticism, mind you, is probably the equivalent of a large gulp of castor oil!

'Words are, of course, the most powerful drug used by mankind,' wrote Rudyard Kipling. Words have a *real* effect. To live creatively it helps to speak creatively. The words you choose speak volumes about who you are now and who you will become. By altering the words you use you can create new melodies and you can sing new songs. As with thoughts and beliefs, if you become more mindful of your words you can nourish and enrich your world. Change words; change worlds!

'SELF-TALK'

Talking to your Self is fine—we all do it; the time to worry is when you hear a reply!

Michael Furber

The most important conversations you hold in life are the ones you hold with your Self. Deep within you there is a 'silent voice' or 'inner voice' that nobody else hears. This voice conducts a continual conscious and unconscious inner t[ace]te-a-t[ace]te dialogue—at this very moment it may be commenting, 'I can't hear my silent voice,' 'Where's my inner voice gone?' 'I already knew that,' or, 'Does this mean I'm mad?'

'Self-talk' causes and affects your Self-image, your thought patterns and your belief system. You speak to your Self at a (conservative) average of 120 words a minute—that's 7,200 words an hour. Even when you sleep, your inner voice can still be in animated flow, especially when you are dreaming. These words will influence, colour and confirm the way you feel, think, believe, see and live.

Every moment of your day you are saying something to your Self. You may be praising your Self or putting your Self down; you may be consoling your Self or criticizing your Self; you may be inspiring your Self or inhibiting your Self; you may be being your own best friend or your own worst enemy. Whatever you say consciously or unconsciously will be heard and will either be helpful or harmful.

A gentleman by the name of Mark came to see me for one-to-one psychotherapy. Mark was then in his late twenties, single, out of work, living with his father, suffering from irritable bowel syndrome and clearly quite anxious. Mark was so critical of himself. On our first session I heard him affirm 'You idiot' or use the word 'idiotic' at least eight times in an hour and a half. 'Who do you think was the first person to tell you you were an idiot,' I asked? 'My father,' he replied.

The clue I got to ask Mark this particular question was that he insisted on affirming 'You idiot' rather than 'I am an idiot'. If you say something to your Self, and it really comes from you, you will mostly begin your statement with 'I'; when, however, you say something to your Self and it really comes from a parent, a teacher, a peer or a past experience, you will invariably begin with 'You'. Listen to your Self for a while and really hear where what you say comes from—is it from you or from someone else?

Mark had wanted to play professional football for West Bromwich Albion. On one occasion, at the age of 14, he had to leave the pitch during a game to go to the loo. 'You idiot,' his father told him. I explained to Mark that he could only hope to control his irritable bowel syndrome if he was prepared to drop the 'idiot script' and start to 'Self-talk' more helpfully. *When you speak, your body listens, and so does the whole of your being.* Mark moved out of his father's place soon after our fourth session together, and his life moved on, too.

'BUT, IF'

Our words are a faithful index of the state of our souls.
St Francis de Sales

Your 'Self-talk' is littered with conscious and unconscious suggestions, affirmations and beliefs that limit your natural capacity for abundant happiness and personal fulfilment. Day by day, moment by moment, we all of us impose limits on our 'wonder-full', 'joy-full' potential by saying, avowing or commanding otherwise. These 'internal memos', as I call them, help run your entire life—rewrite the memos and you can rewrite every chapter of your life.

My psychotherapy practise has taught me that most people are far too hard on themselves and far too Self-critical. This destructive Self-judgement often manifests by way of destructive 'Self-talk'. Examples of 'critical talk' frequently include the words 'must', 'should' and 'ought': 'I mustn't let anyone down;' 'I should be better than this;' 'I ought to know;' 'I shouldn't be resting, I ought to be working' are a few common Self-recriminations.

There is also such a thing as 'obstacle talk'. This talk is made up of words, phrases and statements that can get in the way of our joy and happiness. Examples of 'obstacle talk' often include words like 'can't', 'difficult', 'impossible', 'hard', 'try', 'tough' and 'don't know'. Many of these words affirm fear, not freedom. By changing 'can't' to 'can' we confront a problem and we create a new possibility.

'Stall talk' describes the sort of messages we send when we are procrastinating, delaying and deferring our actions (and our happiness). Common phrases used in 'stall talk' include 'I hope' instead of 'I can'; 'maybe' instead of 'I will'; 'yes, but' instead of just 'yes'; 'if only' instead of 'OK'; 'next time' instead of 'now' and 'tomorrow' instead of 'today'. Saying you will get around to things means you will only ever live your life in circles.

Agree to eliminate one word from your everyday vocabulary that you know limits your freedom of joy. Replace this word with an appropriate, expansive word that is without limitation. Replace, for instance, 'I can't' with 'Let's see'. Do this for 21 days and you will find that *as you improve your language you can improve your life*. A conscious change changes your consciousness. As we change our consciousness, we change our world.

'JOY SPEAK'

One word of joy transforms a dull old man into a bright young boy.

One of the first creative growth games I introduce to newcomers at my Laughter Clinics is a 'Language of Joy' exercise in which each participant is asked to identify and relate to a partner everything he or she finds joyful about life. The game lasts a mere five minutes, which I think is not a lot when you consider that by the time you are 30 you have lived more than 15,768,000 minutes. Alas, for most people this joyful time is at least five times too long—one minute of joyful communication exhausts people—people have even fallen asleep during this exercise!

There is, I believe, a highly infectious mental and social disease at large in our society which I call 'gloomeritis'. Most people find it easier to talk about misery than joy;

they are more comfortable relating to sadness than to gladness. *Whatever you focus on, flourishes!* (See 'Image', above). The more you talk about gloom, the more gloom there is to talk about; conversely, if you begin to explore a language of joy you will discover more joy to speak about. Try it!

For every one word of joy in the English language there are over 40 words for misery—for every one year of peace in our history there have been over 40 years of war. Is there a correlation here, I wonder? We are so eloquent, so poetic when we relate to misery and gloom; the words so often dry up when we attempt to speak of joy, blessings, delight and wonder. To live joyfully it helps to cultivate a language of joy: the words you send out create the world you get back. Let's give joy a little more airtime!

And when we are happy, what then? We use strange phrases like 'I'm *terribly* glad to see you,' 'I've done *awfully* well,' 'I'm *frightfully* happy' and 'I had a *hell* of a time.' When we are in agreement with our friends we use odd phrases like, 'I *can't* argue with that,' 'You're *not* wrong' and 'You *can't* be faulted.' Things we like are '*dead* good', and the greetings we give each other sound like sermons on a life sentence: 'How are you?' we ask; the replies come thick and fast, 'Not too *bad*', 'Can't *grumble*', 'No *complaints*' and '*Surviving*'. When are we going to thrive?

GOOD NEWS

Kind words towards those you daily meet,
Kind words and actions right,
Will make this life of ours most sweet,
Turn darkness into light.

Issac Watts

By the time an average child reaches the age of 18, he or she will have been praised, encouraged, congratulated and told 'Well done' an average of 30,000 times. More than half of these helpful affirmations will be over by the time the child has had his or her third birthday. By contrast, the average 18 year old will have been criticized, discouraged, reprimanded and told 'Don't be silly' well over 225,000 times. Never miss an opportunity to communicate good news—we all of us need to hear more of it.

The mass media of radio, television and the press do not help matters. When I trained to become a journalist my working bibles were entitled *Bad News, More Bad News* and *Even More Bad News*. I first worked for a local paper where my editor was never more miserable than when there was no bad news. 'People buy bad news,' he said. 'Bad news travels fast,' he told me. 'Good news does not sell,' he affirmed. Any good news he received was always automatically relegated to about page eight and beyond.

One day, with about two hours to go before press, the atmosphere in the office was particularly tense: we had no bad news for the front page! It was early June, there was a mini-heatwave and one of the sub-editors was angling for a picture of a model bathing in a field of sunflowers. The editor was about to agree when news arrived of a local car crash which had either badly injured or killed a young mother and her baby. The whole office cheered! We had our front page! 'See if they've died yet,' ordered the editor. That day I resigned my ambition to be a journalist.

At the Laughter Clinic we play a creative growth game called 'Highlights' in which we relate good news to one another, as a group. The key questions are: 'What are the seven best thing that have happened to you this week?' and 'What is the best thing that has happened for you today?' So simple! This game trains the mind to look for, attract and enjoy good news. What you communicate is what you connect with.

Another creative growth game we play at the Laughter Clinic is called 'Bouquets'. This game encourages you to send sprays of praise, compliments and good favours wherever you go. This is such fun, and so rewarding! Experiment with 'Bouquets' your Self. You will be energized, recharged and magnetized by the experience. As a Danish proverb goes, 'Kind words don't wear out the tongue.' Imagine if every individual gave just one compliment to someone today—this planet of ours would be improved for ever, and our world could never be the same again.

SAY SO

First say to your Self what you would be; and then do what you have to do.

Epictetus

You do have a say in your life. Whatever you say is taken into account and you do receive a return. Words are deeds;

there is no such thing as a wasted word. What you say, and how you say it—rhythm, pitch, intonation and energy—can command you, both consciously and unconsciously.

Every word you speak is an affirmation. One of the most empowering actions you can perform is to own everything you say with 'I' rather than the common habit of saying 'You'. Fitz Perls, founder of Gestalt Therapy, observed that many people prefer to use 'You' instead of 'I'. For example, a man may say of himself, 'When you're nervous you feel tense,' instead of 'When I am nervous I feel tense.' Don't speak for others, speak for your Self. Own what you say.

You will assert your Self well if you express your Self well. Affirmations can help. Two words—'I can'—make a difference. Encouraging 'I can' affirmations can help liberate who you really are and who you want to become—they can brighten up Self-image, upgrade thought patterns and polish belief systems. The following 'I can' affirmation sequence is best practised in accordance with the guidelines on pages 60-62. To add power to these affirmations don't just think them, say them out loud. You can, of course, make 'I can' affirmations of your own, and put them into practice.

Inhale: *Say: 'I can be more than good enough.'*
Exhale: *See it, feel it, believe it.*
(Repeat three times)

Inhale: *Say: 'I can be calm, relaxed and confident.'*
Exhale: *See it, feel it, believe it.*
(Repeat three times)

Inhale: *Say: 'I can rise to my best on every occasion.'*
Exhale: *See it, feel it, believe it.*
   (Repeat three times)

Inhale: *Say: 'I can bring out the best in others.'*
Exhale: *See it, feel it, believe it.*
   (Repeat three times)

Inhale: *Say: 'I can love my Self.'*
Exhale: *See it, feel it, believe it.*
   (Repeat three times)

Inhale: *Say: 'I can be even more loving to others.'*
Exhale: *See it, feel it, believe it.*
   (Repeat three times)

Inhale: *Say: 'I can be kinder to my Self from now on.'*
Exhale: *See it, feel it, believe it.*
   (Repeat three times)

Inhale: *Say: 'I can be kinder to others from now on.'*
Exhale: *See it, feel it, believe it.*
   (Repeat three times)

Inhale: *Say: 'I can help my Self even more.'*
Exhale: *See it, feel it, believe it.*
   (Repeat three times)

Inhale: *Say: 'I can help others even more.'*
Exhale: *See it, feel it, believe it.*
   (Repeat three times)

Inhale: *Say: 'I can be stronger than ever before.'*
Exhale: *See it, feel it, believe it.*
   (Repeat three times)

Inhale: *Say: 'I can be more the real Me.'*
Exhale: *See it, feel it, believe it.*
   (Repeat three times)

3

FULFILMENT

HAPPINESS

I am happy because I have made up my mind to be happy.
                                                    Donald Gardener

We are all of us, at heart, happiness-orientated and joy-directed. To be happy, joyful and prosperous is our natural condition; to build a happy, joyful and prosperous life is our natural, automatic goal. Each and every day of our lives we wake up with at least the hope of experiencing today a little more happiness, joy and prosperity than we had yesterday.

I believe that everything we do is designed deep down (partly consciously and partly unconsciously, depending on our level of Self-awareness) to make peace with our Self, to realize our innate happiness and to fulfil our Self. How we go about this depends much on how we perceive and relate to 'happiness'. For example, do you see happiness as a good job, a loving relationship, voluntary service or a new BMW car?

Life is a relationship to happiness. What you perceive as happiness will be what you set out to realize, achieve and get close to. You grow, change and evolve through life as your experiences of happiness grow, change and evolve. Through experience you alter your perceptions of happiness and, thereby, you alter your perceptions of life, love and the universe! As your perceptions of happiness change, you change.

This lifelong quest for personal happiness is more a *rediscovery* than a *discovery*. It is not selfish; it is liberating— *for everybody!* I guarantee you now that, as you realize and give birth to your innate happiness and your true Self, you will find you cannot help but respond automatically and instinctively to the call of humanity and to the collective quest of other people's happiness. *True happiness inspires true humanity.*

HARMONY

Happiness is harmony; unhappiness is discord.

In my book *Stress Busters* I describe a 'harmony principle' which states, 'happiness, wholeness and healing begin with harmony.' Without harmony there can be no happiness. Without harmony there can be no agreement, no acceptance, no peace; body, mind and soul experience unrest and *dis-ease* when harmony slips away. Harmony is the flower, happiness is the fragrance. If you allow harmony to blossom, you will have your happiness.

Physically, your body craves harmony—the medical term is 'homoeostasis'. When healthy, your muscle groups tense and relax in chorus, your sympathetic and parasympathetic nervous system sing in tune, your digestive organs make a pleasing melody between acids and alkalines, and your lungs and circulation dance in time with both oxygen and CO_2. Your body is happy and most efficient when it is in harmony. 'Health is harmony; disease is discord,' wrote Aristotle.

Emotionally and spiritually, too, you crave harmony. Happiness cannot happen without harmony. For instance, you cannot be happy at work if you are not in agreement with your boss or your colleagues; you cannot be happy at home if you are unsettled and not in tune with your loved ones; and you cannot be happy with friends if you are upset and at odds with them. The challenge is not to find happiness; it is to restore harmony. Harmony heralds happiness.

The most important harmony of all is Self-harmony. Life is good when you feel good about your Self. You are much better equipped to deal with the events of life when you are in tune and not at odds with your Self. Personal poise, inner calm and 'Self-centring' help to replenish and restore your natural resources of positive Self-image, appropriate thought, creative belief management and effective communication.

I do not believe that happiness can be defined as the absence of sadness, tears, pain, hurt, suffering, etc. Rather, I think that true happiness embraces, integrates and accepts all the emotions. Ultimately, *happiness is being in harmony with whatever is happening, wherever you are, whomever you are with and with whatever you have*. For instance, if you support and work *with* your tears you will restore harmony and happiness more easily than if you suppress and work *against* your tears.

Although not all events in life are happy, every event can, over time and if handled well, increase your happiness. Everything can add to your strength, enhance your wisdom and make the person you are more mature. Indeed, everything is here to benefit you, even sadness, if you are prepared to look for and work *with* the benefit (see

'Rainbows', below). The challenge of happiness is aligning your Self to the harmony and to the 'helpful' that is potentially in everything.

HAPPINESS IS...

If you don't know what happiness is, how will you know if you are happy?

Picture the following scene: the Caliph Abdelraham, dressed in white, bearing a sceptre in one hand and a piece of parchment in the other, stands before an open gathering of his joyful subjects who have amassed in their thousands outside the temple. The Caliph raises his hand to the sky. As if by magic, the noisy, babbling crowd smoothes into a still sea of silky silence. The Caliph rolls out the parchment and begins to speak:

I have reigned above 50 years in victory or peace, beloved by my subjects, dreaded by my enemies and respected by my allies. Riches and honours, power and pleasure have waited on my call, nor does any earthly blessing appear to have been wanting to my felicity. In this situation, I have diligently numbered the days of pure and genuine happiness which have fallen to my lot: they amount to precisely 14.

Each time I read these words I am filled with laughter. In a single moment, the beloved Caliph blows away, for all those who would really listen, many of the myths of happiness. He confirms that riches, honours, power and pleasure do not automatically create happiness. In fact, nothing has an innate power to *make* you happy, other than your Self.

Here are a few more myths for you to blow away:

- Your best friend can't make you happy.
- Mum, Dad, brother, sister, friend, husband, wife and baby cannot make you happy. No person has that power other than your Self; others can encourage you to be happy, but they cannot make you happy.
- Your new dishwasher can't make you happy.
- The same goes for hoovers, washing machines, televisions or pressure cookers. Think about it. A household object may make your life easier, but no household object has an innate power to make you happy.
- Other people's happiness can't make you happy.
- It is certainly helpful and inspiring when the people you love are happy, but that does not automatically mean you get to be happy. Similarly, another person's misery cannot make you miserable. You choose.
- The future won't make you happy.
- Time can't make happiness for you. You are more likely to be happy in the future if you work at happiness in the present moment. Happiness is not in the moment; it is in the mind.
- Your next success won't make you happy.
- Status, position, fame and money can be great experiences; great as they are, they have destroyed more lives than they have saved. Success is happy when you realize that success, of itself, cannot make you happy.
- Happiness is nowhere in particular.
- There is no one town, city or country in the world where every resident is automatically happy just

because they live there. A beautiful environment is an enormous help, but happiness still depends on you.

- Happiness is not good luck.
- Even if luck really existed, it still could not bring you happiness. Nothing brings you happiness; happiness is something you bring out of your Self. Happiness is about pluck, not luck.
- Happiness is not the absence of sadness.
- An absence of sadness cannot assure happiness. The happiest people alive use their sad feelings as opportunities to create strengths, lessons, blessings and growth. To be sad is not implicitly bad.
- Happiness is not a result of doing anything.
- Your happiness is not a result of doing; it is a consequence of being. Nothing you do will automatically confer happiness. Happiness is not a way of doing; it is a way of being.
- Happiness is not a result of having something.
- Owning a car, keeping a pet, possessing a house or even 'having' a partner will not create happiness for you. Clinging to a 'must have' usually leads to pain. Owning nothing but enjoying everything still can't make you happy, but it's a jolly good start.

THE HAPPY YOU

Foresee happiness; forgo hurt: the more you look for the happy you, the easier it is to find the happy you.

Mary was in her early fifties, a Catholic who had been married to 'him' for 25 years. She had three sons, all of whom lived away from home. When I first met Mary she

94

apologized for being 'frightfully early' (by a full three minutes!) and for having sticky hands because of the warm weather. Mary apologized for everything; she even apologized for apologizing too much.

'I am called Mary,' she told me, 'but I think my real name is Mary Martyr.' Mary had devoted her life to her husband and family. Each and every day she washed, cooked, cleaned and kept the men happy. At the time she didn't mind what was happening because she didn't know what was happening. After her youngest son, Steven, moved home, it became apparent to her that she had no life of her own. Initially she was sad, then she was furious, and then she became determined.

'God willing, I have maybe 20 more years in me. What shall I do?' Mary wanted to make up for the wasted years, and yet whenever, as she put it, 'I catch my Self enjoying my Self', she felt 'terribly guilty'. Mary was not used to being happy. I asked her one day, 'Mary, what does the happy you look like?' She paused. There was a long silence. First she smiled. Then she coughed. She shifted in her seat. Finally, her eyes spilled tears. 'I don't know, Robert. I can't see it. I just can't see it,' she replied.

What does the happy you look like? Can you see your Self in future becoming more happy, or do you think that your happiest days are already over? What do you see for your Self, and what do you see in your Self? Remember, perception is often a Self-fulfilling prophecy (see Part II, 'Image'). If you cannot foresee your Self as happy, you may well have to forgo being happy. Mary could only begin to experience peace and happiness once she gave her Self the permission to be happy. She had to see it before she could believe it. Take a moment for your Self and write, paint, draw or scribble a portrait of the happy you. Consider:

- What does the happy me look like?
- What does the happy me think like?
- What does the happy me believe in?

- How does the happy me express my Self?
- How does the happy me behave each day?
- How does the happy me enjoy my Self?

- Where does the happy me live?
- Where does the happy me work?
- Where does the happy me relax?

- What does the happy me do differently now?
- What does the happy me aim for in life?
- What does the happy me do for other people?

Make a personal happiness forecast. Create an image of the happy, fulfilled you. This is not a fantasy; this is for real. Hold the image in meditation at the beginning of the day for five to 10 minutes. Enhance the meditation with appropriate affirmations if you wish. Create your own role model: be who you would most like to become. Enjoy the journey, every day, and recognize that every experience is here to help you shape, evolve and give birth to a fuller, happier you.

A HAPPY FAITH

If you believe it is too good to be true, will it last?

Sally described her Self as, 'the lady who had everything'. She was in her mid-thirties and had been married for five years to 'the most delightful man in the world'. She had recently given birth to their second son. They were very well off financially. The new house was an absolute dream. 'I feel so absolutely blessed and I should be very happy,' she told me, 'but I'm miserable. I've never been so miserable in all of my life.'

Up until meeting her husband, Geoff, Sally's life had been a daily struggle. At 29, she was convinced she had been 'left on the shelf'. Money had always been a problem. Work was unfulfilling. Relationships had always been disappointing—the men in her life never stuck around. Meeting Geoff was the beginning of a complete life transformation. Everything was perfect, 'more than I ever dared imagine'. The only thing in Sally's way was her misery.

Sally believed everything she was experiencing was 'too good to be true'. Her present experience was disproving a lot of her past beliefs, hence the inner conflict. Essentially put, Sally was suffering from 'fraud guilt'—she felt guilty for having so much happiness. Together, we set about changing Sally's belief system. In particular, I helped her to see that her abundant happiness was not depriving anyone else of happiness.

Take a pen and paper and write down every negative belief you have about happiness. Begin, 'My most negative belief about happiness is...' Relax, breathe easily, and allow

97

the thoughts to flow without editing. Give your Self a full 15 minutes, no less. Then, take another 15 minutes to jot down every positive belief you have about happiness, beginning, 'My most positive belief about happiness is...'

Your negative beliefs about happiness are the principal obstacles between you and your birth right of abundant happiness. Although most of these negative beliefs are unconscious, they have a conscious effect on your Self-image, your thought patterns, your communication and your daily behaviour. Each and every day of your life you set out to prove and affirm your beliefs, positive and negative. You live by your beliefs.

Negative Beliefs	Positive Beliefs
Happiness doesn't ever last	Happiness can be ever-lasting
I'll lose the happiness I find	Happiness can be for ever
Happiness is too good to be true	Happiness is real
Happiness doesn't exist	Happiness is for everyone
Happiness is over-rated	Happiness is as great as I make it
I don't deserve happiness	I deserve all the happiness I receive
Happiness is for others	Happiness is for me
Happiness is for the lucky	Happiness is a choice
My happiness deprives others	Happiness is not rationed
My happiness hurts others	My happiness helps others
It will end in tears	Happiness breeds happiness
It'll be more miserable afterwards	Happiness is kind
Happiness is too difficult	Happiness is easy and natuiral
Happiness is rare	I can find happiness every day if I look for it
Happiness is never as good as I expect	Happiness can be as good as I make it

In my experience, negative beliefs about happiness often outweigh positive beliefs by about three to one. How did you do? How much happiness can you handle?

Sally came from a 'God-fearing' family as opposed to a 'God-loving' family. Her father was a Priest in the Church of England. Many of her negative beliefs about happiness were inherited from her family. She had swallowed the idea that punishment follows happiness. Where have you got your negative beliefs from? Play detective, and understand where from and how your negative belief system has developed.

HAPPY AFFIRMATIONS

Happiness is a state of mind in which our thinking is pleasant a good share of the time.

Dr John Schindler

You can be as happy as you make up your mind to be. If you want to attract greater happiness in your life, resolve to make as many opportunities as you can to affirm happiness, think happiness, look for happiness, recite happiness, sing happiness, believe in happiness and spread happiness. Make happiness a way of travelling and not some final far-off destination. Work at happiness; do not wait for it.

Willingness is the key. You must be willing to be brave, to experiment a little and to think differently. If you are not willing, it will not happen. From 0–100 per cent, how willing are you to be happy today? Name a percentage. Are you 40 per cent willing, 60 per cent willing or 90 per cent willing? Or are you 100 per cent willing to be happy but you know that it is hardly possible? Check out your beliefs. Your negative beliefs are outdated. If you make a change today, today need not be the same as yesterday.

The following affirmation sequence was created for Sally. This sequence may serve as inspiration for your own 'I Can Be Happy' statement. Once again, I advise that you follow the affirmation guidelines on pages 60-62 so as to get maximum benefit from this very simple, powerful exercise. Sally worked at this sequence twice a day, every day, for 21 days. Her work made the affirmations work. I wish you good fortune.

Inhale: *Affirm: 'I do deserve all the happiness I receive.'*
Exhale: *See it. Feel it. Believe it.*
Inhale: *Affirm: 'I can let go now of the erroneous belief that I do not deserve to be happy.'*
Exhale: *See it. Feel it. Believe it.*
(Repeat three times)

Inhale: *Affirm: 'My happiness can last for as long as I want it to.'*
Exhale: *See it. Feel it. Believe it.*
Inhale: *Affirm: 'I can let go now of the erroneous belief that my happiness never lasts.'*
Exhale: *See it. Feel it. Believe it.*
(Repeat three times)

Inhale: *Affirm: 'I can find happiness every day if I look for it.'*

Exhale: *See it. Feel it. Believe it.*

Inhale: *Affirm: 'I can let go now of the erroneous belief that happiness is rare.'*

Exhale: *See it. Feel it. Believe it.*

(Repeat three times)

Inhale: *Affirm: 'My happiness can benefit everybody I meet.'*

Exhale: *See it. Feel it. Believe it.*

Inhale: *Affirm: 'I can let go now of the erroneous belief that my happiness hurts others.'*

Exhale: *See it. Feel it. Believe it.*

(Repeat three times)

Inhale: *Affirm: 'Happiness is my birthright—it is easy and natural.'*

Exhale: *See it. Feel it. Believe it.*

Inhale: *Affirm: 'Happiness is a choice I choose to make.'*

Exhale: *See it. Feel it. Believe it.*

(Repeat three times)

SUCCESS

One's religion is whatever he is most interested in, and yours
is Success.

Sir James Barrie

Every healthy human being wants to be a success! It is in
our nature to want to flourish, bloom and thrive.
Consciously and unconsciously, you and I orientate all of
our reserves and resources towards our perceived version of
success. You are doing it right now! So am I! And the good
news is that we are each of us endowed with such
astonishing creative potential that we have the power and
authority to write, direct and star in our very own success
story in life.

The word 'success' derives from 'succeed', 'succession'
and the Latin *succedere* which means 'to go on well'. For
every moment of your life, the spirit whispers to the soul,
the soul whispers to the mind, and the mind whispers to
the body 'Grow, develop and unfold; grow, develop and
unfold.' You are here to enrich your Self and the world
around you. You are here to prosper in adventure. You are
here to give birth to your successful Self. We are all
winners; no one need lose.

Our society usually limits the word 'success' to the world of career, work and business. Our society worships work before life: work is celebrated; life is tolerated. Society champions the *human doing*, not the *human being*. There is also, however, such a thing as a successful education, successful friendships, successful marriages, successful homes and families, and even successful worship. Work is important; life is more important.

ASPIRATION

If you have not worked out what success is, how will you be able to work for success? And how will you know when to celebrate?

John had set out to make a fortune in life. He aspired to success. His ambition was success. Success was his goal. Before long, colleagues at work began to tell John he was a success. Promotion meant success, so John gained promotion after promotion. Eventually, his manager told him he should go for the position of European operations manager; John did it. By the time John came to see me, he was earning over £150,000 a year, had a jet-set life, a wife, one child and a mansion. 'I am a success,' he told me, 'but I don't feel like a success.'

John was an alcoholic. His family life had collapsed. Friends, there were none. John was miserable. 'Every time I thought the next promotion would do it,' he told me, 'I kept hoping the next success would make me happy.' John had thought if he worked more he would be more successful, more happy. The alcohol was a help, then a hindrance. John had worked *at* success, but he had not worked *out* success. He had tried to find success; he had never defined success. He was clearly still looking.

We all set out to make a fortune in life. Everyone prepares for success; only a few are prepared to work out what success is. For years, I have had the pleasure of running *Personal Empowerment Programmes* for the National Health Service, local government, the BBC and the organization Business in the Arts, for instance. Again and again many of the problems I encounter, such as low moral, poor motivation, no fixed goals, absenteeism, inadequate communication and high job turnover stem from a poorly defined and poorly communicated concept of success.

From my experience, I have found that eight out of 10 people go to work with an unclear idea of what success is. I once, for instance, trained 56 Social Services managers in 'Stress Busters', 'Time of Your Life' and 'Team Spirit' courses. When I asked them for their definition of success at work, only two of the managers had a ready-made definition. If the manager doesn't know what success is, how can the team know? As for success outside of work, none of the managers had a ready-made definition. If the mother or father doesn't know what success is, how can the family know?

A well-defined idea of success can be a life-enhancer and, in the case of John, a life-saver: you will manage your time better, you will motivate your Self better, you will handle apparent failures better, you will enjoy better energy, you will have more direction in life, you will gain greater results and you will inspire support and confidence in what you do. With a clear definition of success, you can win; without it, you are lost.

Your definition of success will be unique to you,

because you are unique. Take pen and paper and draw, paint, write or scribble your ideas of success. The more you work it out, the better you can work at it:

- Success at work is...
- Success at work requires...
- Success at home is...
- Success at home requires...
- Success in life means...
- Success in life requires...
- A successful friendship is...
- A successful friendship requires...
- A successful relationship is...
- A successful relationship requires...
- A successful family is...
- A successful family requires...

Add any other variables you like.

Success is only ever nourishing when you *feel* a success. The ultimate success is not about what you do, it's about who you are. Success is not the achievement of a human doing; it is the realization of a human being. You can't 'do' successful, you can only 'be' successful. Living successfully is all about living authentically. The more you labour at learning about the real you, the more easily you can give birth to the real you—only then will you get to feel happy and only then will you get to feel a success.

Each day of my life I prepare a *Successful Day* sheet for guidance and inspiration. At the top of the sheet I write the words of Albert Einstein:

> Try not to become a man of success but rather try to become a man of value.

We are naturally drawn to what we value. A successful life is all about supporting, upholding and being inspired by all that we find valuable in life. The more you know what you value, the more you will know the feeling of success.

Finally, if you really want to be successful, do not make success your goal. John made that mistake. Success is not a goal; it is a reward. Success is not about position or status, it is not a commodity or a financial statement; success is a feeling. Aim, therefore, at what you value, at what you believe in and at what inspires you. Make your inspirations your aspirations. Be real to your Self, unfold your real Self and you will experience automatically the real feeling of success.

WORTH

Self-worth determines personal prosperity.

There comes a point with almost all of my clients when I ask them, 'How much are you worth to your Self?' In particular, I want to know how much time, energy and effort a client will invest in him- or her Self. I also want to know how much care, consideration and love my clients feel they can afford to show themselves. You are worth what you believe you are worth.

'What do you feel you can afford?' I will ask. I have known clients who have had heart attacks and then walked back into the jobs that almost killed them because they felt they couldn't afford to look for a new position; I have had clients on tranquilizers who declined essential dietary help because they felt they couldn't afford to bother changing their diet; I have had young mothers on the verge of breakdown because they felt they couldn't afford space or time for themselves.

Your successes are a product of your Self-worth, your Self-image, your thought patterns, your belief systems, your Self-expression and your personal behaviour. You are the key to the world's door. The American poet, Henry Longfellow, put it well:

> Not in the clamour of the crowded streets,
> Not in the shouts and plaudits of the throng,
> But in our Self, are triumph and defeat.

The following 10 guidelines may well help polish your key!

1. *Define success*. The more you know about it, the more you will know how to go about it. For every minute of life you take to define success, you save hours, days, weeks and years trying to find success.

2. *See success*. Set a goal and see your Self being successful at achieving that goal. Each and every day, envisage your Self as a success. Aim, focus and keep seeing it happening.

3. *Value success*. Value your Self. Value your talents, skills and abilities. Value your time, your effort and your rest. Value your goals. Value inspires motivation; motivation effects energy. Energy gets things done!

4. *Affirm success*. Success is an 'I can' attitude and an 'I will' determination. Affirmations can help facilitate a real feel for success. Your success is an 'estate of mind'.

5. *Believe success*. Believe in your Self and believe in your success. Affirm your positive beliefs about success;

dispense with your negative beliefs about success. A practical faith will fortify you.

6. *Speak success*. Be sure that the language you use is 'success-friendly'; beware of 'fail talk'. Watch out for the 'ifs', the 'onlys', the 'whens' and the 'buts'. Communicate so as to inspire.

7. *Act success*. Always ensure that whatever you are doing you are acting 'as if' you are a success and 'as if' you are going to be successful. Everything can add to your success if you take it that way.

8. *Effect success*. Do not wait to be successful; work at it. Everything responds to the law of cause and effect and the law of like attracts like—including success. Work at success and success will work for you.

9. *Stick to success*. The path to success leads on from the road to failure. In other words, failures often lead to successes, especially if you know how to take failure. Let your failures inspire your successes.

10. *Take responsibility*. Take responsibility for your successes and your failures; no 'blamerizing'! Excuses will be your executioner. Be responsible and you will find life will be responsive.

FAILURE

The secret of success is to know how to survive failure.

Failure is not fatal—it just feels that way sometimes! That's what I had to keep telling my Self when I first embarked upon a writing career. I was genuinely astonished each time I received the standard two-line letter from an editor telling me my masterpiece was unpublishable! I became a brilliant failure, though. I was so good at failure that I finally failed 71 times before my first book was accepted for publication.

I decided that failure is not bitter if you do not swallow it. Although a failure feels like for ever, it is fleeting. Each time I failed, I would celebrate it as a success. Seventy-one times I enjoyed a meal out on my failure! I felt *down* each time I received a rejection slip but I never felt *out* because I always ensured that at least three editors had one of my books at any one time. My chief 'success philosophy' is, 'Give people every opportunity to say "Yes" to you.'

A fear of failure can so often overwhelm a desire to succeed. If you do not understand failure, failure will undermine you. We all of us must graduate from the school of failure if we are to gain entrance into the university of success. Failure does not stand in the way; it is the way. Nobody begins as a success: failure is the fire that forges the metal in us to succeed. By learning how to fail well you learn how to succeed well. Here are some thoughts on failures:

- *There are only lessons.* Every event in the universe offers a teaching. Look for the lesson and you can then pass the grade. There are not failures, only lessons. Lessons are everywhere if you 'see' them.
- *Failures teach success.* Every failure is a step to success if you take it that way. By learning how not to succeed you are automatically learning more about how to succeed. Every failure is a lesson in success.
- *Failures are not 'bad'.* Nothing is implicitly 'bad' or 'good'; it's what you do with something that makes it

so. If you take it that failure is 'bad', 'bad' is what you get—look for the good news in every failure.

- *Failures can be 'good'.* Every event in the universe can be helpful if you take it that way. Defeat can stand you on your feet; endings make way for beginnings; the worst trial can set you free. Make your failures work for you, not against you.

- *Failures are not final.* Failure is not falling down, it is staying down—and even then all you are doing is learning another lesson. Perhaps the ultimate lesson is that you are always free in life to make another chance for your Self. Are you willing?

DETERMINATION

Success nourished them; they seemed to be able, and so they were able.

Virgil

Kevin is a first-class production engineer with a major television broadcasting company. He has had 15 years' experience, commands respect from everyone, takes on managerial duties, enjoys senior responsibilities—yet he has not had a promotion for 12 years and he is on a wage that falls far short of his talents. 'I fail at interviews,' he told me, 'I go to pieces and my hopes fall apart.'

After a series of long discussions, it became apparent that, although Kevin was valued by his colleagues, he did not value himself. He belittled his talents, made minor his accomplishments and overlooked his skills. His Self-depreciation was impoverishing his life. His low Self-worth was fuelled by a low Self-belief. I suggested to Kevin that it was about time he gave his old Self-disregard a new look.

Another major problem was that Kevin openly admitted he no longer believed he would pass an interview again. He also believed the blame for his failure lay with an ex-boss of some 10 years ago who had 'made me tight', to use Kevin's words. Deep down, we discovered Kevin also believed he did not deserve any more success than his dad, who had worked in the same field for over 40 years, had achieved. Kevin idolized his dad.

Your beliefs make successes 'impossible' or 'possible'. When Kevin finally got this message, he got his promotion and he got his rise. Pick up a pen and paper now and make a list of your own beliefs about success. Begin, 'My most negative belief about success is...' Give your Self a full 15 minutes. Then begin again, for another 15 minutes, with, 'My most positive belief about success is...' Here are a few common examples:

Negative Beliefs	Positive Beliefs
I am not good enough	I can be good enough
I can't do it	I can do the best I can, moment to moment, for ever
I won't get there	I can continue to move forward for ever
I don't deserve it	I can deserve everything I make and everything I receive
Success is short-lived	I can enjoy successes again and again
Success is hard	I can be successful easily, effortlessly and naturally
Success is selfish	I can allow my success to benefit everyone

111

Success corrupts people	I can be unspoilt by success and by failure
Success is for the rich	I am rich at heart
Success is greedy	I can be generous with my success
Success changes a person	I can change for the better with my success

As with happiness, your beliefs about success will have first been inherited from your parents and other family members. Later you will have picked up other beliefs from teachers, peers, school experience, initial work experience and meaningful relationships. The road to maturity and personal fulfilment requires that you off-load other people's negative beliefs and fill up on your own positive beliefs. Success is a triumph of belief.

ENRICHMENT

The more you value your Self, the more valuable your life will become—to you and to others.

You have to make a success of your Self before you can make a success of the world. Your Self-image, your thought patterns, your belief systems, your Self-expression and your personal behaviour will either *set up* or *upset* your chances of success. Success is not created; it is nurtured. Success is already in you; all you have to do is learn how to extract it. Your natural, inner resources can make you rich.

You can enrich your life if you first enrich your Self with a helpful vision, constructive thoughts, supportive beliefs, faithful Self-expression and consistent action and behaviour. The following *Personal Enrichment Programme* is a simple affirmation sequence that you may like to experiment with. Do modify it: make it your own, or make one of your own. This sort of programme is best practised following the affirmation guidelines on pages 60-62.

Inhale: *Affirm: 'I can be good enough.'*
Exhale: *See it. Feel it. Believe it.*
    (Repeat three times)

Inhale: *Affirm: 'I can be successful.'*
Exhale: *See it. Feel it. Believe it.*
    (Repeat three times)

Inhale: *Affirm: 'I can enrich my life.'*
Exhale: *See it. Feel it. Believe it.*
    (Repeat three times)

Inhale: *Affirm: 'I can prosper every time.'*
Exhale: *See it. Feel it. Believe it.*
    (Repeat three times)

Inhale: *Affirm: 'I can value my Self even more.'*
Exhale: *See it. Feel it. Believe it.*
    (Repeat three times)

Inhale: *Affirm: 'I can grow and develop*
    continually.'
Exhale: *See it. Feel it. Believe it.*
    (Repeat three times)

Inhale: *Affirm: 'I can give birth to my Self, fully.'*
Exhale: *See it. Feel it. Believe it.*
   (Repeat three times)

Inhale: *Affirm: 'I can fulfil my Self again and again.'*
Exhale: *See it. Feel it. Believe it.*
   (Repeat three times)

Inhale: *Affirm: 'I can feel my Self successful.'*
Exhale: *See it. Feel it. Believe it.*
   (Repeat three times)

R A I N B O W S

My heart leaps up when I behold
A rainbow in the sky:
So was it when my life began;
So is it now I am a man
So be it when I shall grow old,
Or let me die!

William Wordsworth

Sometimes the challenge of day-to-day living feels more like an ungainly wrestling match than an elegant, graceful dance. The ground beneath our feet can be unsteady and unpredictable—it is as if we are walking on mud, not solid earth. And when the sun shines all around us, even then there are times when it can still be raining in our hearts. 'The web of life is of a mingled yarn,' wrote Shakespeare, 'good and ill together'.

Light emerges from the darkness, sunshine from behind the rain, warmth rises from the cold and the blossoms of spring evolve from the bareness of winter. Life, the human adventure, is a fragrant mix of beginnings and endings, emptiness and fullness, happiness and sadness, laughter and tears, wonder and woe. Life is everything; and we will eventually experience everything at least once.

Everything adds to your life; everything adds to who you are. Sadness defines happiness; failure can inspire success; illness can teach you about health; emptiness can encourage you to search for fulfilment. *Everything helps everything.* In my psychotherapy practice I encourage people to discover for themselves that pain, hurt and sadness do not have to be destructive; they can be constructive. After the rain falls, we get to see rainbows.

PEACE

> I take it that what all men are really after is some form or perhaps only some formula of peace.
>
> *Joseph Conrad*

Guy had recovered from agoraphobia about five years ago; now he was suffering a relapse. I agreed to meet him at his home one day. 'It's going to be a long hard struggle,' he told me, 'but I've done it before and I'm sure as hell going to get there again.' Guy was in fighting mood and he was determined to, in his own words, 'do battle', 'kill it off' and 'win once and for all'.

I asked Guy what had worked for him previously. 'Sheer guts,' he told me. He had made himself go out. He told me how he would shake, sweat, tremble and be ill, but he would still make himself leave the house at least once a day. He used affirmation, visualization, meditation and anything else he could find to defeat his agoraphobia. No one could fault Guy's courage, determination and persistence.

Guy was making war with his agoraphobia; I suggested to him he might consider making peace with it. Guy was trying to silence his agoraphobia; I encouraged him to listen and learn from it. Guy perceived agoraphobia as an enemy; I personally believed it was a 'disguised friend' offering protection and help. Guy was initially more interested in *warfare* than in *why-for*. Eventually we both of us went to school, not war. Guy worked with the agoraphobia, not against it.

So often we make an enemy of illness, failure, pain and hurt. We negotiate war; we negate peace. We sound the battle cry; we fail to listen. We try to get back to the way we used to be instead of using events to move forward to a new (and possibly better) way of being. What if the 'problem' was not meant to harm us, but help us? What then?

WRONG

For as long as you make something wrong, it cannot have a chance to go right for you.

Much pain is caused or exacerbated by making things 'wrong'. Whenever you object to something you create resistance, not remedy. 'Pain exists only in resistance; joy exists only in acceptance,' wrote the twelfth-century Persian poet Rumi, 'Joyful situations which you do not accept become painful. There is no such thing as a bad experience. Bad experiences are simply the creations of your resistance to what is.'

Sometimes people focus so much on what they feel is 'wrong' that they obscure anything that might be 'right'. As a result they concentrate on the problem, not the solution; they become engrossed in the hurt, not the healing. In other words, for as long as you make something 'wrong' it will oppose you and will work against you. You are stuck.

Carol's father had died, aged 54, while on holiday in Greece. The whole event was a nightmare for Carol. She had not seen her father for the six months previous; she forgot to ring the day he left; she had to go to Greece to identify the body; she even had to pay for the body to be shipped back to England. Carol was still grieving; her father had died more than two years before.

I encouraged Carol to see that her father's death was 'sad' but not 'bad'. Death is not 'wrong' or 'right'; it simply 'is'. Carol was making her father's death 'wrong'. According to Carol, he shouldn't have died at 54, he shouldn't have died abroad, she should have rung him, she should have cared more, and she shouldn't be left all alone. Carol described her father's death as 'unfair', 'cruel' and 'unjust'. Her attitude was not helping her to accept or come to terms with her grief.

Carol also made her own feelings 'wrong'. 'I shouldn't still be feeling this way now,' she told me. I explained to Carol that it was because she was resisting her feelings that they were persisting. I suggested that her father's death was a sad event and that she should express the sadness rather than suppress it and repress it. If you keep it in, you can't let it go. 'It's OK to feel sadness; sadness is not wrong,' I told her.

The more you increase your resistance to life, the more you increase your pain. The more you make pain 'wrong', the more your pain will be prolonged. When you make your feelings 'wrong' you tend to resort to short-term avoidance strategies, both conscious and unconscious, such as suppression, repression, denial, rationalization, displacement or intellectualization. *Whatever you avoid follows you around.* Face it; make friends with it; integrate it.

Own your feelings. Hurt, pain and sorrow are not harmful if you own and accept them; they can only harm you if you resist them, fight them and make them 'wrong'. The lid always leaks—do not put a lid on your feelings. Do not block your feelings; let them flow through you. Express your Self; do not suppress your Self.

GOOD

There is nothing either good or bad, but thinking makes it so.

Shakespeare

Your judgement, your perception and your attitude determine whether or not something is 'sad', 'bad', 'wrong', 'awful' or 'disastrous'. Your position, your stance and your view will also determine whether or not you see the positive, envisage hope, discover benefits or find opportunities. If things are looking 'bad', shift to a 'good' point of view.

Everything has a value. We can learn from everything. We can learn from pain, for instance. 'Even pain pricks to livelier living,' wrote Amy Lowell. During times of sadness we can choose to care for ourselves even more. Hurt can increase our resolve to rise again and be happy again. 'A wounded deer—leaps highest,' wrote Emily Dickinson. If you value an experience, you will better extract its value.

Whatever you experience, assume it is for the good.

Believe that everything is, directly or indirectly, on your side. Recognize that everyone is, ultimately, your teacher and your helper. Say to your Self, 'This event/person is potentially good for me because...' Look for opportunity; search for an opening; seek an advantage. 'It's them as take advantage that get advantage in this world,' wrote George Elliot in her novel *Middlemarch*.

Acknowledge burdens; pursue blessings. Feel the pain; locate the gain. Adversity, like anything else, is an education. If you cannot externally govern an event, govern your Self internally through the event. Remember, it is not what happens to you in life that counts, it is what you do with what happens that counts.

ACTION

It's wonderful what one person can do when he is dedicated to doing it.

Edward Hale

In my book *Stress Busters* I added to the well-known *fight or flight* response theory of stress by developing the *freeze* theory. Very often when people experience pain, hurt, sadness or failure they will also experience a desire to stay where they are. This 'cease and freeze' reaction inhibits flow, arrests change and prohibits progress.

One of the biggest causes of stress in life is doing nothing about your stress. Procrastination, worry, indecision and doubt are natural stress symptoms; if they persist they trigger fatigue, frustration, sleepiness and powerlessness. Emotions of despair and anxiety inevitably follow. Alas, no amount of anxiety has ever once cleared up a personal problem.

120

Many people block their own healing and delay their own happiness by focusing on anxiety and forgoing action. In particular those people with low Self-esteem will feel they cannot act. These feelings are fiction, not fact. Self-neglect can lead to Self-destruct; deep down it can even feed our 'death urge'. Instead of helping your Self out of a situation, 'freezing' in this way may lead you to try to drink your Self further and further into a hole, or smoke your Self further in, eat your Self further in or even starve your Self further in. Are your actions helping you or harming you? Are you being your own best friend or your own worst enemy?

Such Self-destructiveness has to give way to Self-creation. Even if you don't feel like it, if you are willing to invest in your Self you will enrich your Self. Even if you don't think 'I can', if you are willing to start affirming 'I can' you enhance your chances of success. And even though you don't believe in your Self, if you are willing to change what you believe you will see a change in how you live.

Ideas of 'if', 'but', 'only' and 'after' need to heed the actions of 'now'. 'We become just by performing just actions, temperate by performing temperate actions, brave by performing brave actions,' said Aristotle. Don't wait for life to get better: it won't. It is *you* that must get better; then life will change as a consequence.

BREATHE

The harmony of the lungs support the harmony of life.

Mental 'make wrong' and emotional resistance tend to create uncomfortable sensations in the body. Events that are 'hard to stomach' often show up as knots in the solar plexus; a 'broken heart' often causes tightness in the physical heart; an unwillingness to move can create muscle stiffness in the legs and feet; and a short, shallow, irregular breathing pattern is one of the first symptoms of distress and dis-ease. If we do not flow, our breathing does not flow. As a result, we fail to assimilate things physically and mentally, we fail to digest things physically and mentally, and we fail to eliminate things physically and mentally. The body feels what the mind feels; the body remembers what the mind remembers; the body blocks what the mind blocks.

Many holistic therapies such as massage and body work, Yoga, Tai Chi, reflexology, shiatsu and Qi Qong are physical therapies and psychotherapies in that they help to shift mental and physical resistance and clear the blocks. These techniques, together with rebirthing, vivation, meditation and various other techniques also help people to learn a deep, full, flowing breathing pattern.

Full, Flowing and Free

As a child, your breathing was naturally full, flowing and free. For five minutes in the morning and five minutes at night, allow your Self time and space to rediscover and redevelop this most natural breathing pattern.

Allow every breath to be full, flowing and free. Let there be no gap between inhalation and exhalation. Do not force the breath: *let the breath breathe you.* Hold on to nothing; let go of everything. You are aiming to create your own breathing space.

Inhale: Affirm: 'Full, flowing and free'.

Exhale: See, feel and believe you are full, flowing and free.

Repeat for five minutes. Be gentle on your Self when you finish—your energy will have shifted and you will need a moment or two to balance and adjust before you continue with your day.

The next time you feel stressed, check your breathing and undoubtedly you will find it has collapsed. People will often hold their breath and even stop breathing for a time when facing unpleasant feelings. This collapsed breathing can create unpleasant physical tensions which will increase mental and emotional tension. If you keep the breathing free, you will be free.

If you breathe through your 'uncomfortable feelings' instead of blocking them or making them 'wrong', you will integrate and make peace with your feelings more quickly. If you restore a full, flowing, free breathing pattern, your mind, body and situation will begin to shift and to move again. Pain hurts when it cannot flow; let it flow and the pain will go. Harmony in your lungs will support harmony in your life! Try it.

HEALING

Life is very simple: You are alive to heal, to be happy and to make harmony with everything and everybody—leave nothing and no one out!

You are a healer. Your body is a Self-healing mechanism. You heal, replenish and rejuvenate your Self constantly. Physical, emotional and mental healing can be greatly enhanced if you resolve to make the most of what comes and the least of what goes. In other words, if you surrender, accept and work with, not against, what you have and what is, you will come to terms with any apparent conflicts.

Life is for you, not against you. Below I summarize my *Rainbows* approach to psychotherapy:

- *Own your feelings*. Express what you feel, do not suppress it, repress it, deny it or intellectualize it. Remember, the lid always leaks.
- *Don't fight it*. Health is harmony; harmony cannot happen while there is a war on. Flow with it, don't fight it. Do not resist; surrender.
- *Don't make it 'wrong'*. You are a child of the universe, everything in the universe is here to help you, not harm you. If you make your life 'wrong', it will not be able to go 'right' for you.
- *Identify the 'good'*. Look for the gift in everything; identify the lesson; discover the benefit; and make an opportunity to allow whatever is happening to add to the good in your life. Watch for a rainbow!
- *Be willing to act*. The universe rewards conscious action. Maybe the action is to rest and be, rather than to get

124

up and do. Be willing to act and you can change the scene you are presently starring in.

- *Be willing to breathe*. A collapsed breathing pattern promotes collapsed thinking. A full, flowing, free breathing pattern allows the whole of your being to be full, flowing and free again.

- *Affirm your health and your happiness*. Self-image, thought patterns, belief systems and personal expression and behaviour can all be upgraded so as to help you to heal and grow. Do not miss the opportunity to affirm your healing.

LAUGHTER

Laughter is a child's best friend.

Laughter is your birthright. To laugh is an essential human need, a universal elixir and a necessary part of every person's travelling pack in life. Like an ointment, laughter can soothe you, invigorate you and uplift you. Laughter is for consolation, celebration and jubilation. The most cherished moments of life are those when our spontaneous joyful laughter sounds out like a bell from a church tower.

To laugh for no reason at all is one of the sweet gifts of childhood. Children love laughter! As children we needed no reason to laugh. Laughter is natural; it needs no explanation. Conditions are not necessary; laughter is, at its purest, unconditional. The unconditional child feels free with laughter because he or she trusts laughter, trusts love, trusts life. The world-weary adult is, on the other hand, often mistrustful and consequently fears laughter.

Social psychology research shows that children laugh on average 150 times a day; adults laugh on average only six times a day. During an average day, a child will smile 400 times; an adult will smile no more than 15 times. Research also shows that a child will spend on average six to eight hours a day at play; an adult averages 20 minutes a day at play. Children rarely, if ever, feel guilty about enjoying themselves; one in two adults say they experience some guilt when they catch themselves having fun.

On average, a child will pick up a crayon, a pencil, an art-brush or a pair of dancing shoes over 50 times a week; an adult will only indulge themselves in a creative pursuit maybe two or three times a week. Children will spend on average over 30 hours a week with friends; adults will spend less than eight hours a week with friends. Research shows that the average person makes three times more friends in the first 18 years of life than in the next 50.

So many adults witness a demise of delight in their day-to-day living. The innate ability to wonder at the world so often wanes as we make our way into adulthood. The sheer surprise of being a *human being*, of existence itself, soon wears off as we become more and more preoccupied with the struggle to be a human doing. We lose our wonder; we need to resurrect the child of wonder in our hearts.

LAUGHTER MEDICINE

Laughter is a great medication: it is the only medicine you can overdose on that actually helps you live even better to tell the tale.

One of the very first people to walk through the doors of my NHS Laughter Clinic was a gentleman by the name of Edward. Edward had a worried sort of look on his face that suggested either he was about to confess something, faint, or walk back out the door again. 'Is this the Laughter

Clinic?' he asked nervously, 'Yes it is,' I replied. 'Is it free?' he asked. 'No wallet, just willingness,' I told him. 'Good,' he said, 'I'd like to learn how to stop laughing'.

Edward was in his late sixties, retired. Much of his day he spent either gardening for people or working down at his own allotment. He had been sent to the Clinic by his wife, who had read about it in a local newspaper. 'I seem to laugh in all the wrong places,' he said, smiling, 'My wife gets a bit annoyed because I'm always whistling and cheerful. I just can't help it; I was born like it I suppose.' 'We all were,' I replied.

Edward told me: 'No matter how bad things get, I always find some laughter'. He then asked: 'Is this healthy?' I suggested to him that his natural inclination for laughter and optimism probably made him one of the most highly medicated men alive! Laughter is a medication. To laugh aloud is a little like jumping on the spot: the whole of your body (particularly your torso) is exercised, stretched and toned. It only takes 15 seconds of continuous belly laughter to cause most people to break out in a sweat!

After the exercise of laughter, the body enjoys a 'cooling-off' period which relaxes the muscles, soothes the nerves, deepens and frees the breathing, enhances circulation and reduces or stabilizes blood-pressure. When we laugh, the body's natural pain-killing chemicals, endorphins, are released into the body together with other hormones that actually help speed up healing. Best of all, medical research proves that laughter can even enhance the function of your immune system.

HUMOUR THERAPY

To take humour can help you to take heart.

When I first met Mina she looked like the saddest person on Earth. Mina was in her forties, divorced, living on her own with her two young daughters. Two years previously she had experienced a near fatal heart attack—the ground from beneath her feet had been swept away in an instant. Since then, Mina had never been quite sure where she stood in life. She trusted nothing; she feared everything. Nothing was solid anymore.

'My little daughter shouted at me, "Mummy why don't you ever smile anymore?" ' Mina recounted. 'It is true I have been very, very sad for a long time, but it nearly broke my heart when my little daughter shouted at me. I need help.' Mina was, in effect, waiting for a second heart attack. She didn't dare open up, smile or live again for fear of having her happiness taken away again. Mina was maintaining the belief that, 'I'll be punished for my happiness.'

The Laughter Clinic encourages people to trust in happiness again. It also encourages people not to wait for happiness but to work for it. I dared Mina to be happy again. Together we questioned her unconscious erroneous beliefs. First, I urged Mina to enjoy a 10-minute 'happy spot' each day, then a 'happy hour' each day and, finally, a whole day of unashamed happiness! Again and again, we proved to each other that happiness is not a punishable offence—it is a birthright.

Laughter is a liberator. Humour can help you to challenge your fearful, irrational belief systems and thought patterns. Above all, laughter can be the trigger that stops making things 'wrong', 'bad' or 'awful'; laughter lends perspective, adjusts points of view and helps integrate and resolve feelings of fear, doubt and tension. 'When we can begin to take our failures non-seriously, it means we are ceasing to be afraid of them. It is of immense importance to learn to laugh at ourselves,' wrote Katherine Mansfield.

Laughter is a form of courage—it is a Self-preservation reflex. To laugh at your Self and to laugh at your situation can help you to face fear, address doubt, relax tension and reduce anxiety. Laughter also has a way of helping you to see the best in the 'worst', to find good in the 'bad', to make the most of the least, and to put right whatever is 'wrong'. Laughter, creativity and resourcefulness are a great threesome—they will perform for each other and for you, too.

RE-CREATION TIME

Life is the ultimate game! To live without fun, without laughter and without play would be the ultimate shame!

Have you ever experienced the joy of watching two young cats at play? They scamper to and fro, first fast then slow. They run, they pounce, they leap and they roll. Under and over, one this way and one that, backwards and forwards they go. What energy! What agility! What creativity! Every possible option is explored again and again.

Life is a creative act. You and I are at our most creative when we are at play, enjoying the world and having fun. We first learn to create and re-create our lives through play. As children our greatest learning came from laughter, fun and play: we learned about friendship, team-work and working together well; play helps to develop skills of confidence, communication and co-operation. The day was filled with play, and we were filled with joy.

One of the chief aims of the Laughter Clinic is to test the therapeutic power of play. I do all that I can at the Clinic to encourage people to play with life. Playfulness will bring out your finest qualities. Make a conscious decision to go out to play today. Make whatever you are doing your play. Allow play to enhance your commitment to whatever you are doing. Become a child again and wonder at all that you do.

When was the last time you went out to play? If you have a problem, get creative! Life is play! You can play victim or victor; toss your problem over and look, under and over, into the past, into the future, now, one month from now; entertain positives and negatives; amuse your Self with possible benefits and opportunities; engage your Self in a hunt for a lesson or value; search out a gift for your Self in all of this. Play it out.

Laughter and play encourage lateral thinking: humour naturally encourages a person to explore fresh avenues, new ideas, alternative routes and different angles. Laughter can make a difference: it can help us see differently, think differently, believe differently and communicate and behave differently. Laughter and play help us to break through, not break down.

DIVINE COMEDY

Joy is divine—it is the melody of a wonder-full life.

It is not necessary for you to prove your devotion to life, or to others, by frowning a lot and looking serious; joy is enough! 'One laugh of a child will make the holiest day more sacred still,' wrote Robert Ingersoll. Joy is your birthright, your heritage, your passport and your final destination. You entered the world a 'bundle of joy'; receive and radiate joy! This is our primary purpose; it is our most authentic act. Make joy your philosophy and your practise.

Most religions tell us we are here to suffer. In my experience I have found that suffering is usually an experience of the ego, coming out of a desire to own or out of a feeling of separation. Joy, on the other hand, is an experience of the universal Self, of the desire to set things free, of harmony and connection. 'One hallmark of freedom is the sound of laughter,' wrote Harry Ashmore. Let everyone be; set everyone free. Own nothing; enjoy everything.

Suffering is not a sin or punishment for joy; it is what happens when we are separated from joy. Laughter is for giving; laughter is forgiving. It was Nietzsche who wrote, 'An inability to take seriously for any length of time their enemies, their disasters, their misdeeds—that is the sign of the full strong natures.' Laughter is restorative; it takes us back to joy; it sets us free; it reminds us of the Divine Comedy.

WONDER-FULL AFFIRMATIONS

Love is laughter's highest inspiration.

After the Laughter Clinic had been running for a few months, I began to experiment with what I called my 'Wonder-full Affirmation' series. I even created an affirmation sequence called 'Living Wonder-fully' to help me write this book faithfully, honestly and to the best of my ability.

Many affirmations begin with 'I can', 'I am' and 'I will'. I decided to create an alternative series of combined verbal and visual affirmations that begin with joyful statements such as, 'I can enjoy', 'I can flow', 'I can happily' and 'I can love'. If something is enjoyable it automatically becomes easier to do. Enjoyment is a motivation and an inspiration.

The following Wonder-full Affirmation sequence is designed for pure enjoyment. Please feel free to experiment and play with the affirmations. The whole sequence is best performed to the guidelines on affirmation practice given on page 60. Affirmations can be enjoyable: the rewards and benefits are certainly enjoyable. Enhancing and enriching your life need not be excruciating; it can be entertaining.

> Inhale: *Affirm: 'I can enjoy even greater courage in my life.'*
> Exhale: *See it. Feel it. Believe it. Enjoy it!*
> ***(Repeat three times)***

Inhale: *Affirm: 'I can enjoy even greater integrity in my life.'*
Exhale: *See it. Feel it. Believe it. Enjoy it!*
(Repeat three times)

Inhale: *Affirm: 'I can enjoy even greater love in my life.'*
Exhale: *See it. Feel it. Believe it. Enjoy it!*
(Repeat three times)

Inhale: *Affirm: 'I can enjoy even greater happiness in my life.'*
Exhale: *See it. Feel it. Believe it. Enjoy it!*
(Repeat three times)

Inhale: *Affirm: 'I can enjoy even greater friendship in my life.'*
Exhale: *See it. Feel it. Believe it. Enjoy it!*
(Repeat three times)

Inhale: *Affirm: 'I can enjoy even greater prosperity in my life.'*
Exhale: *See it. Feel it. Believe it. Enjoy it!*
(Repeat three times)

Inhale: *Affirm: 'I can enjoy even greater inspiration in my life.'*
Exhale: *See it. Feel it. Believe it. Enjoy it!*
(Repeat three times)

Inhale: *Affirm: 'I can enjoy even greater peace in my life.'*
Exhale: *See it. Feel it. Believe it. Enjoy it!*
(Repeat three times)

Inhale: *Affirm: 'I can flow with courage.'*
Exhale: *See it. Feel it. Believe it. Enjoy it!*
(Repeat three times)

Inhale: *Affirm: 'I can flow with integrity.'*
Exhale: *See it. Feel it. Believe it. Enjoy it!*
(Repeat three times)

Inhale: *Affirm: 'I can flow with love.'*
Exhale: *See it. Feel it. Believe it. Enjoy it!*
(Repeat three times)

Inhale: *Affirm: 'I can flow with happiness.'*
Exhale: *See it. Feel it. Believe it. Enjoy it!*
(Repeat three times)

Inhale: *Affirm: 'I can flow with friendliness.'*
Exhale: *See it. Feel it. Believe it. Enjoy it!*
(Repeat three times)

Inhale: *Affirm: 'I can flow with prosperity.'*
Exhale: *See it. Feel it. Believe it. Enjoy it!*
(Repeat three times)

Inhale: *Affirm: 'I can flow with inspiration.'*
Exhale: *See it. Feel it. Believe it. Enjoy it!*
(Repeat three times)

Inhale: *Affirm: 'I can flow with peace.'*
Exhale:*See it. Feel it. Believe it. Enjoy it!*
   (Repeat three times)

4

CELEBRATION

PURPOSE

Perhaps the ultimate end of human existence is in being able to respond to the beauty, the everlasting peace, the glorious wonderment of the mystic world itself.

Norman Vincent Peale

Why would you want to take a train that was going to a place called 'nowhere'? What would be the fun in watching a football match without goal posts? Why would anyone want to run in a race with no route and no finishing line? Could you imagine taking part in a debate without a point? Who would want to go to the theatre to see an unfinished play? Why would anyone bother to go to a concert hall to hear a symphony without a finale?

You are purpose-built. You are designed with intention. You are goal-directed. You are meaning-full. You are the director of your life. As director, you can choose the play, set the scene and alter the script. You can decide who has the staring roles, you can explore and create new meanings, you can interpret events—you can even determine how to begin and end.

To determine a direction in life that is authentic to who you are (and who you aim to become) is an essential human need. To have a cause, to adopt a purpose, to make your own meaning and to discover your own truth in life are as basic as knowing how to roll out of bed each morning. A direction in life is the vital difference between being lost and found. Without a point, you become blunt. A life without aspiration is a life without inspiration.

The psychologist and philosopher Carl Jung once wrote, 'About a third of my cases are not suffering from any clinically definable neuroses, but from the senselessness and aimlessness of their lives.' I would say that well over two-thirds of the people who come to my own psychotherapy practice experience feelings of pointlessness, purposelessness and subsequent powerlessness. Futility fuels dis-ease and dis-harmony.

'The wisest men follow their own direction,' wrote Euripides. The happiest people do also! Waiting to see 'what life offers', 'what the future holds' or 'how things go' will take you nowhere. Destiny is either a conscious choice or an unconscious fate. Be conscious of what direction you choose. Beware, *if you do not consciously set your own direction in life, plenty of people will give you their directions to follow!* They may be happy; you won't be. Choose consciously; choose well!

CAUSE

What use do I put my Soul to? It is a very serviceable question this, and should frequently be put.

Marcus Aurelius

I only ever met Margaret twice. During our first consultation together, Margaret told me she had worked at the same school for almost 35 years, 18 of which she had been headmistress. Three months previous, Margaret had reached what she called her 'sell-by date'. Margaret had retired. The new school year had now begun; Margaret felt like her life was over. She was clearly distraught and disorientated.

As well as losing her job, Margaret recently had had to close the local youth club which she had run for over 10 years, due to lack of funds. 'I'm a lost cause,' she wept. I suggested, 'You are now presented with a fabulous opportunity to discover a new cause.' I then told her, 'I have homework for you!' Together we worked through a simple goal-setting formula that was to revolutionize her life.

When I saw Margaret coming up the path for her second consultation she wasn't walking, she was waltzing! 'I'm here to tell you that there is life in the old girl yet,' she proclaimed. Margaret told me she had completed her goal-setting on the very first night. A fine example! Margaret decided, among other things, she was going to go back to school! Her subject: philosophy. Margaret had a purpose again; Margaret was alive again.

Basically put, there are two main categories of stress in life: *survival stress* and *identity stress*. Survival stresses involve 'staying alive' pressures such as keeping a roof over your head, paying the bills, having socks and shoes and making sure you have enough money to pay for the cornflakes. Identity stresses are about questions such as 'Who am I?', 'What is the point of my life?', 'Where am I going?' and 'How do I get there?' These common crises of identity can be just as life-threatening as the survival stresses.

'He who has a *why* to live for can bear almost any *how*,' wrote Nietzsche. A good cause can animate, preserve and fortify your whole being. A purpose in life fills you with motivation, energy, morale, power, vision and strength. Persistence, commitment and Self-determination are rewards that bring further rewards of their own. Your universal creative potential rises and manifests in response to the heights you set for your Self.

It was Sir Winston Churchill who wrote, 'When great causes are on the move in the world, stirring all men's souls, drawing them from their firesides, casting aside comfort, wealth and pursuit of happiness in response to impulses at once awe-striking and irresistible, we learn that we are spirits, not animals.' As you reach out, so you extend your Self.

Every child born on Earth is endowed with enough energy to make opportunities to evolve a higher Self, to attune to a higher consciousness and to perceive and manifest a higher vision. To give birth to the divine universal, creative potential within is a fundamental higher goal of all humanity. Ultimately, everybody helps everybody all the time, directly or indirectly, to love Self and to liberate humanity. This is the ultimate goal of goals.

Every personal cause is also part of a collective cause. 'No task, rightly done, is truly private. It is part of the world's work,' wrote Woodrow Wilson. You and I, we are not separate individuals living in isolation; we are connected, we are universal! Every authentic personal act the world witnesses take you, me and all humanity closer to the ultimate fulfilment, which is to exist and co-exist in ever-evolving peace, joy and creativity. Make your crusade—make your cause take effect!

MEANING

> There is no meaning to life except the meaning man gives
> his life by the unfolding of his powers, by living
> productively.
>
> *Erich Fromm*

Every person tries to create meaning, order and signif-
icance in life. Basically put, life must mean something to
you and to others if you are to live fully with wonder and
joy. A life without meaning is an existence without point
or purpose and, although I can't actually prove it, I believe
that more people have died of futility than of any
common virus or ailment.

The Austrian psychiatrist Dr Viktor E. Frankl was a
survivor of the Nazi concentration camps. His horrific
experiences taught him that a man or woman can survive
any hardship so long as his or her meaning of life remains
intact. After the war, Dr Frankl founded a school of
psychology called *logotherapy*, based on the Greek word
logos, which means 'meaning'. In his book *Man's Search for
Meaning* he writes:

> Man's search for meaning is the primary motivation in his
> life and not a 'secondary rationalization' of instinctual drives.
> This meaning is unique and specific in that it must and can
> be fulfilled by him alone; only then does it achieve a signif-
> icance which will satisfy his own will to meaning.

Much of twentieth-century social psychology research
proves again and again that human beings need a purpose,
an aim or a meaning for which to live. We are happy to be
living, but we are even happier when we are actually living
for something. The inspirational Helen Keller once wrote,

'Many persons have the wrong idea of what constitutes true happiness. It is not attained through Self-gratification but through fidelity to a worthy purpose.'

An eternal whisper beckons us again and again to sow a seed, plant a tree or bear fruit. As creators, we carry a divine responsibility to give and add to the creation we are a part of. We are here to give birth, in the broadest sense, to a new generation of life. Many people testify to an almost religious feeling of wanting to leave a memorial that adds to the meaning of this world. We are here to make an impression.

You do not *find* a purpose or a meaning in life, you *create* it. Purpose and meaning are not given to you by life, they are made by you for life. You decide, for instance, if what happens means 'disaster' of 'opportunity'; you choose if something means 'good' or 'bad', 'right' or 'wrong'; and you determine if an event means 'end' or 'new beginning'. You are a 'meaning-creator' because you choose the context and you decide your frame of mind. *You make the meaning, and the meaning makes your life.*

AIM

The soul that has no established aim loses itself.

Montaigne

Do you know what the principal aim of your life is? Are you aware of what is the most exciting motivation of your life? Have you any idea what prompts you to get out of bed each day? Without a well-defined aim, it is very difficult to know whether or not you are on target or off course. Progress, growth, development and achievement are not measurable if there is no aim. Without an aim you have missed before you even draw.

You are, right at this moment, heading somewhere. Your whole life is a wonder-full journey with countless ports of call. There is a momentum to every moment which is, like a wind on the high seas, blowing your ship across space and time. Wouldn't you like to know where you are going? If you set sail and control the rudder you can even enjoy the luxury of choosing where you would like to go! With an aim, your travel can be faster, further and more fulfilling.

Below are a few a exercises which will help you identify your own motivations, aspirations and aims. The more you consider them, the more you will improve your aim. Also, as you explore and learn more about your Self, your aim will become clearer and more authentically yours. Enjoy your Self!

- List 10 things you would most like to be in life. Identify characteristics, traits and personality aims.
- What would you like to be? Who would you like to become?
- List 10 things you would most like to do in life. What actions, achievements and accomplishments would you most like to fulfil in life? What targets are you aiming for?
- List 10 things you would most like to change in your life. Be realistic. How could you upgrade the quality of your life? What could you do to enhance your happiness?
- List 10 things you would most like to have in life. Think physical, mental and spiritual. What sort of a

house are you aiming for? What sort of reputation do you want? What sort of skills would you like?

- List 10 things that you would like to contribute to life. What is your crusade? What will you donate to life? How will this world be different because of you?
- List 10 things that you are prepared to make a stand for in life. What is your crusade? What are you prepared to support? Where do you stand?
- List 10 things you would like to make happen by the end of the week. And when you are ready, do the same for the end of the month and the end of the year. You will keep your aim straight if you first set your sights on a target.

GOALS

Make life a goal or you make your life a gaol.

Anonymous

How can you achieve a goal you have never even set? How can you tell if you have hit a target that does not even exist? Which way is forward and which way is back if you have no direction? We are all of us travelling somewhere in life, and yet, astonishingly, only one person out of 50 makes a conscious decision to set directions and destinations for life. Most people do not make the most of their lives because they mostly have no conscious goal, direction or purpose.

I believe there are five essential blocks that stop people from setting goals in life:

1. *People do not understand the value of goal-setting.* A well-set goal takes you halfway to where you are going. You are inspired, energized and charged. You can manage time, organize your Self and prioritize well. You can monitor, motivate and encourage your Self well. Apparent failures are easier to handle if you keep the end in sight. Your purposefulness will empower your every move.

2. *People do not know how to set goals.* I went to school and to college for a total of 16 years, and in that time not one hour was devoted to the most important skill of all: goal-setting. This was probably because people do not value setting goals. One simple goal-setting technique is all you need to revolutionize and metamorphosize your life. The first goal you must aim for is to set aside time to learn the technique!

3. *Goal-setting takes a lot of time.* We live in an instant, quick-made society which demands everything now, this minute. Goal-setting is a very deliberate process that requires many hours of exploration, planning and monitoring. Goal-setting takes a lot of time; it also, however, saves a lot of time. Wrong turns, cul-de-sacs and dead ends are easier to avoid if you carry the map of a well-defined goal.

4. *People are conditioned to accept they won't reach their goal.* Many people shy away from goal-setting because of 1) a poor Self-image, 2) a lowly thought pattern, 3) a pessimistic belief system and 4) inadequate Self-expression. They cannot see themselves being successful; they do not think they are able; they refuse to believe they can; and they talk as if they will inevitably fail (see Part II, 'Image'). Beware your power

to create disappointing Self-fulfilling prophecies.

5. *People are afraid of both failure and success.* The fear of failure, rejection and disappointment only ever escalate the amount of failure, rejection and disappointment we experience. *Remember, fear brings on that which you are afraid of* (see Part III, 'Success'). Many people also fear success because success means altering an out-dated Self-image, thought pattern, belief system or behaviour that affirms, for instance, 'I don't deserve to win,' 'I'm not good enough' and 'It won't happen to me.' Set goals for the joy of setting goals — choose this as your motive.

The very best goals are those that aim to build up your universal, creative resources of character and strength. Therefore, anything you can do to fortify your Self-image, liberate your thoughts, enhance your belief system and inspire your personal behaviour will create dividends for all of your life. The ultimate goal is to realise the ability to make everything in life an advantage and opportunity for growth, prosperity and fulfilment.

The following seven-step, seven-day goal-setting technique, that I affectionately call 'Seventh Heaven', is an absolute joy to do. Take as much time as you can, either on your own or with people you respect, so as to be as thorough as possible. The more thorough your research, the more complete your results. You may wish to prepare for this exercise with meditation or relaxation so as to be as clear as possible.

'Seventh Heaven'

1. *What?*

   Identify and print goals for every area of your life: work, family, finance, travel, health, relationships, education, spirituality and personal growth. List every conceivable goal—edit nothing at this stage. Put your list of goals away for a day or so.

2. *Which?*

   Prioritize and order the goals that mean the most to you. Discover which goals excite, inspire or motivate you the most. Determine which goals are realistic: a good test is to see if you can visualize a goal or believe in it. It is also vital at this stage to ask your Self, 'Is this goal really my own?'

3. *Why?*

   All human beings are benefit-orientated. The more benefits you can find for achieving each of your goals, the more motivation you will find. Allow the rewards to inspire your every thought and action.

4. *Who?*

   Who can help you? Who may hinder you? Enlist all the support, help and encouragement you can get. Surround your Self only with the people who will affirm your efforts and improve your chances. Communicate your goals only to friends and not to foes.

5. *How?*

   How could you be helping your Self right now to move closer to your goal? This is the moment when you begin to list actions, steps, strategies and efforts. Devise a daily, weekly, monthly and yearly activity sheet to monitor and maximize your 'hows'. Big goals are a product of lots of little steps.

6. *Where?*

   Where are your actions taking you right now? Is what you are doing taking you closer to or further from your goal? *All goals must be measurable.* A goal like 'to be happy' is not measurable. You need to give your Self more information to give your Self more of a chance.

7. *When?*

   All goals require a 'lifeline' (deadline seems a bit miserable!). It is good to set goals for the day, the week, the month and the year. This way you will be getting used to the idea that it is perfectly OK to succeed with goals every day of your life. Everyday success is the best affirmation of all!

Goal-setting is enjoyable chiefly because it is life-enhancing. Goals help you to grow. Your astonishing universal creative potential will rise to the heights you set your Self. Every area of your life can be enhanced by good goal-setting. The more enjoyable you make your goal-setting the more enjoyment you will have along the way. Ultimately, the real rewards of goal-setting are not what you get at the end but who you become along the way.

TIME

Dost thou love life, then do not squander time, for that's the stuff life is made of.

Benjamin Franklin

Based on a few quick calculations, I have worked out that if I live in this body of mine for a full 75 years, a daily eight hours of sleep will amount to an astonishing grand total of 25 years being spent fast asleep! Similarly, I may well find I spend approximately 20 years of my life sitting in an office somewhere making a living. Furthermore, if it takes me 30 minutes to drive to and from work each day, I can expect to spend at least three full years of my working life in my car!

During my 75-year lifespan, an average one hour a day for eating and drinking will amount to four glorious years eating and drinking. I have also worked out that during my complete lifetime I will spend approximately 455 days reading the papers, 340 days having a bath or a shower, 250 days washing up the dishes, 240 days doing the ironing, and over 200 days sitting on the loo! My wife, Miranda, will unfortunately not permit me to print the total time in her life it will take her to get dressed and ready in the morning!

Time is our most precious and valuable resource; it can also be our most costly expenditure. We 'spend time' and we 'buy time'; we 'steal time' and we 'keep time'; we 'mark time' and we 'make time'. We can, if we are not careful, 'lose time', 'fall behind the times', experience 'lean times' and even 'kill time'. We all of us come to understand that 'times flies' and that, ultimately, 'time and tide wait for no one.'

Basically put, time is a measurement of change; it is the fourth dimension of life. A moment in time is 'a unit of life', and life, as such, is a composite of rhythms, pace, cycles, seasons and intervals. Like life, time does not happen *to* you; you make it happen *for* you. Time is tangible—it is yours to govern, manoeuvre and steer. Every hour, minute and second is yours to be won. You have the resources and skill to travel 'in good time'.

For several years now, I have had the privilege of presenting time-management seminars and workshops which I call, 'Time of Your Life'. I begin these presentations by explaining that good time-management is really all about good life-management and good Self-management. A waste of time is a waste of life and a waste of You! Time is the ultimate gift: reverence it! Receive it with joy and dispense it with joy, and surely you will have *the time of your life.*

'LIFETIME'

The time of your life is important; the life in your time is crucial.

When I first met Rachel, she barely had the energy to tell me what she felt her problem was. Here was a woman who was quite clearly exhausted, deflated and unhappy. The bags under Rachel's eyes were the biggest I had ever seen. Her eyes lacked sparkle, her face had no radiance and her skin was an anaemic pale white. Before Rachel had even begun to talk, the tears rolled down her cheeks and over her lips.

Rachel was in her late twenties. She was married to Peter, her childhood sweetheart. Rachel and Peter had three young daughters, aged eight, six and two. Rachel described her Self as a good mother: 'For years I have coped beautifully, and now, with most of the hard work done, I feel I'm about to collapse.' Rachel felt that her main problem was that she didn't really know *what* her problem was. 'That's why I'm here!' she laughed.

Rachel was a full-time mother all day, a part-time wife in the evenings, and a 'no-time' person in her own right. Rachel gave her Self no quiet time, no fun time and no free time. When I first asked Rachel what she did for her own nourishment, it was as if I had spoken in a weird alien tongue: 'There isn't the time,' she replied, looking completely bemused. Together we worked on a project I called 'Lifetime' which aimed to help her create more time in her life and more life in her time.

Your relationship to time faithfully reflects your relationship to life and, above all, your relationship with your Self. Rachel was mean with her time because she was mean with her Self. The only real reason why Rachel could never find the time for her Self was because deep down she was not prepared to give time to her Self.

The 'Lifetime' project is based on a simple premise: if you improve the quality of your relationship with your Self, you will improve the quality of your relationship with time, and *vice versa*.

Step One: Perceive differently. A common cause of poor time-management is poor Self-image. People who see no value in themselves see no possibility of time for themselves. Remember, time doesn't happen *to* you, you make it happen *for* you. Change your perception and you will see a change in you and a change in time.

Step Two: Think differently. If you think of time as an enemy it will always be against you; if you think of it as a friend it will always be for you. 'Time is a kindly God,' wrote Sophocles. Regularly take time to think how you can make 'this time' better than 'last time'.

Step Three: Believe differently. Most people do not control time well because they do not believe it is possible to do so. Also, most people cannot create personal time and space because they do not believe they are worthy or that they deserve it—the guilt would be too much. Check your belief systems.

Step Four: Affirm differently. Beware of how you speak of time. Use affirmations to change how you relate to time. Affirm, 'Time is my friend,' 'Time is my own' and 'I can handle my own time even better today.' Affirm a new relationship to time.

Step Five: *Behave differently.* Experiment from time to time. Play with time: spend time differently; your world will still revolve! Plan time, organize time and monitor time, all the time. Make time your own.

I often call upon audiences at my 'Time of Your Life' presentations to 'fall in love with time'. Cherish your time, honour your time and respect your time. Set time to control time, and you set your Self free. You will make the most of your Self if you make the most of your time, and *vice versa*. This moment, now, is your *lifetime*, for time really is 'the stuff life is made of'.

'TIME OUT'

The voice of Time cries to man, 'Advance'. Time is for his advancement and improvement, for his greater worth, his greater happiness, his better life.

Charles Dickens

Time is a wonderful opportunity: every passing moment offers you a chance to live even more consciously—creatively; each instant in time beckons you to live more fully. Time is your passport to growth and prosperity. The word 'time' evolved from the Old English *tima*, which means 'prosperity', and the Germanic *timan*, which means 'stretch' and 'extend'. This time, now, is your time to unfold and extend your Self!

Time is a measurement of change; it is also an invitation to change. As the clock alters, so can we. As time moves on, so can we. Nothing is permanent in this world, except for change. There is momentum in every moment. Therefore, each moment in time offers you a potential fresh start and a possible new beginning. Time ripens you. 'A man that is young in years may be old in hours if he has lost no time,' wrote Francis Bacon.

Because we spend too much time as human *doings* and not enough as human *beings* we rush time and time rushes us. Will Rogers once wrote, 'Half our life is spent trying to find something to do with the time we have rushed through life trying to save.' Erich Fromm went even further: 'Modern man thinks he loses something—time— when he does not do things quickly; yet he does not know what to do with the time he gains—except kill it.'

The human *doing* in us is so concerned with *quantity of time* that the human *being* in us is often forced to forgo *quality of time*. The human *doing* is preoccupied with death; it reasons that because after a time the body dies, the Self dies too—and so we have only a limited time. The human *being*, on the other hand, is preoccupied with life: it intuits that although after a time the body dies, the Self lives on— and so we have all the time in the world, and more! Strangely enough, concentrating on the quality of time tends to give us more quantity of it anyway.

I have often encouraged clients to take 'time out' from juggling the responsibilities of human *doing* so as to enjoy the riches of being a human *being*. 'Time out' replaces the 'work agenda' of the human *doing* with the 'life agenda' of the human *being*. 'Time out' can be, therefore, 'time in' for fun, enjoyment, relationships, interests, hobbies, exploration, wonder, learning, play, entertainment and laughter, to name just a few.

Regular 'time out' periods add to the 'time of your life' in that they offer rest, relaxation and a perfect opportunity to refresh your Self. 'Time out' helps you to rebound back into life. You do not stop living because you have 'time out'; 'time out' helps you to a greater quality of life than before. 'Time out' is not time wasted; it is, ultimately, time saved and time enhanced. Regular 'time out' also helps to ensure that you run your time and that your time doesn't run you.

FULL-TIME

Life is full of time: if you make the most of your time, it is reasonable to expect you will make the most of your life.

Life is a full-time commitment and a full-time experience— the desired end is to be fulfilled and to have had a full life. The more fully you value your time the more value-full your time will be. Ultimately, the trick is to balance the rhythms, the pace, the cycles and the seasons in such a way as to be in harmony with time, with life and with your Self. There is time for everything:

To every thing there is a season, and a time to every
purpose under heaven:
A time to be born, and a time to die;
a time to plant, and a time to pluck up that which is planted;
A time to kill, and a time to heal;
a time to break down, and a time to build up;
A time to weep, and a time to laugh;
a time to mourn, and a time to dance;
A time to cast away stones, and a time to gather stones together;
A time to embrace, and a time to refrain from embracing;
A time to get and a time to lose;
a time to keep, and a time to cast away;
A time to rend, and a time to sew;
a time to keep silence, and a time to speak;
A time to love, and a time to hate;
a time of war, and a time of peace.

As children, each day was an eternity. The hour was filled with wonder and we were filled with life. 'As we grow old, our sense of the value of time becomes vivid,' wrote William Hazlitt, 'nothing else indeed seems of consequence.' Do you remember how long the summer holidays of childhood felt? Are you aware how quickly the last year has passed? 'It is familiarity with life that makes time speed quickly. When every day is a step in the unknown, as for children, the days are long with gathering of experience,' wrote George Gissing.

When you live life as if for the 'first time' and the 'only time', you encourage your Self to live again creatively, productively and wonder-fully. One of the keys of creative time-management is that *you do not* find *the time for something, you* make *the time*. Similarly, you do not *wait for the* time, you *work at the* time.

Creative time-management is impossible if there is no direction, purpose or goal in life. Goals require planning, schedules, projections, diaries, starting times, review times and completion times. How would you know, for instance, how to prioritize your time if you have limits set in time? To go back to 'time out', it can also be an excellent tool for reviewing, revising and rededicating your Self to the 'time of your life'.

The ultimate aim is to balance out your time, consciously, so that you can live out your time creatively. The Greek philosopher and poet Hesiod penned a book on time-management in the eighth century BC entitled *Works and Days*. In it he wrote, 'It is best to do things systematically, since we are only human, and disorder is our worst enemy.' Timing, synchronicity and harmony are the methods and goals of creative time-management.

Hesiod also wrote, 'Timeliness is best in all matters.' We know instinctively when the time is right to perform an action or a duty. Our intuition, or inner clock, guides us in such a way that we plan and act in harmony with the right moment and right space. Truly, there *is* 'a season, and a time to every purpose under heaven'. When we live in harmony with life, we live 'in time' with life. When we are 'in time' we are 'in tune'.

- *First time.* Maximize the moment. You will only wake up on this day once in your life, for this day will never be repeated again in the whole history of the human race. Keep fresh, keep alive and keep living wonderfully (See 'Today', below).
- *Make time.* Review, revise and rededicate your Self to the 'time of your life'. Record your time, keep your time and enhance your time. Look for 'time-vampires'; discover time-savers. Organize, plan and make the most of your time.
- *Work time.* You can make time work for you if you work at time. Set your objectives; determine your priorities; create a daily schedule sheet; allocate time to each task; set a deadline.
- *Play time.* Play with time—experiment, explore and have fun with time. Take time out to play with your life. The greatest works in life are the fruits of play. Playfulness is the spirit of all great enterprise.
- *Quiet time.* Take time to be, to relax, to release and to rest. Meditate, calm the mind, 'free-wheel' and enjoy the *acceptance* of being a *human being*; let go of the *achievement* obsessions of the *human doing*.

- *Free time*. Set your Self free from time to time. Give your Self personal space and personal time. Retreat, go on sabbatical or holiday. Allow your Self the time to be free to be who you really are.
- *Quality time*. Make the quality of life your goal, not the quantity of life. When was the last time you truly nourished your Self? When was the last time you truly nourished someone else?
- *Extra time*. You are in extra time right now. This moment is extra—resolve to live it extra well!
- *Full time*. Life is a full-time commitment; it is not an occasional fling! To live fully, you must be prepared to devote your Self *time and time again* to life.
- *Life time*. You will make the most of your life if you make the most of your time. Love the time in your life, and you will live 'the time of your life'.

TODAY

What a wonderful thing a day is! Nothing is more highly to be prized than the value of each day.

Johann von Goethe

One minute before sunrise, the egg breaks open and the dragonfly first flutters and then flies. The babbling river and the verdant, lush riverbanks are the dragonfly's temporal kingdom. Each moment is precious to the dragonfly, for one minute after sunset this beautiful creature will lay its lifeform to rest, for ever. Imagine, one day to live, one day to win your freedom! And yet perhaps you and I are no different, for really we only have one day to live: today!

Today is the whole of your life. You have a lifetime of 24 hours (1440 minutes, 86,400 seconds) to experience, wonder, learn, work, relate, love, laugh and play. 'I do not cut my life up into days but my days into lives, each day, each hour, an entire life,' wrote Juan Ramon Jimenez. Yesterday has happened, tomorrow is yet to happen, today *is happening*—are you?

'Each day provides its own gifts,' wrote Martial. Today is a once-in-a-lifetime opportunity—a cosmic sale never ever to be repeated again in the whole history of the

161

human race! Today is on offer—to you! Today brings you great tidings of choices, options and decisions; there will also be wave upon wave of potential opportunities, occasions and openings. Today is your election—you have the right to vote!

One final thought: today, right now, will one day become one of the 'good old days'! To appreciate the past is sublime; to appreciate the present moment is divine! Let your heart beat, 'Today is the best day of my life'—print these words on your every perception, thought, belief, communication and behaviour. Live today the best you can, and your reward will surely be that you have lived your life the best you could.

'AWAKE'

Do not say, 'It is morning' and dismiss it with a name of yesterday. See it for the first time as a new-born child that has no name.

Rabindranath Tagore

In an average group of 100 people, only 20 (one in five) will know with any certainty what the date is today—most people will have to guess and most will guess wrong. Similarly, as many as four people out of 10 will guess the day (Monday, Tuesday, etc.) wrong too. Most people will *get up* today; they will not, however, *wake up to* today.

Waking is a sacred ritual. It is a meditation, an act of worship. The first moment of the day casts an impression on every moment of the day. In truth, every moment can be a 'waking moment' in which you can give birth to a new point of view, a new thought, a new belief, a new

162

communication and a new action. This world of ours is a world of all possibilities. 'To live is to be born every minute,' wrote Erich Fromm.

At the Laughter Clinic we play a creative growth game called 'Rise and Shine'. The object of the game is to create your own inspirational morning prayer or waking meditation. I would like to share with you one of my own:

> Oh Divine Creator of all this Wonder,
> I fill my heart with love and gratitude
> for the joy of Today.
> Today, I pray, I will awake to my own
> divine potential;
> Today, I pray, I will awake to my own
> divine joy;
> Today, I pray, I will awake to my own
> divine truth.
> Today, I pray, I will radiate love and
> I will receive love;
> Today, I pray, I will radiate laughter
> and I will receive laughter;
> Today I pray, I will radiate light
> and I will receive light.
> Oh Divine Creator of all this Wonder,
> Help me to fill my heart with love and gratitude
> even more for the joy of
> Today.

Can you answer this question immediately: 'What did you wake up for today?' One of the reasons why most people *get up* but do not truly *wake up* each morning is that they do not, consciously, have anything much to wake up for. In other words, most people do not have a conscious direction, purpose or meaning to fill their day. A great cause or an inspirational challenge can help us to wake up to our Self and to life (see 'Purpose', above).

Another reason why most people get up but do not truly wake up each morning is that they have misplaced their natural talent to wonder. *To wonder is to live consciously—creatively*. Most people do not live consciously; they are not in present time. To live unconsciously stunts the growth of your consciousness and you are thus denied conscious choice, conscious appreciation, conscious purpose and conscious freedom.

To wonder, as the new-born child does, allows you to awaken, to be aware of and to arise to the wonder-full potential in you and in life. Wonder teaches you that every moment is a creative moment. Today is a new start, a fresh beginning and a unique moment in time. Today is happening for the first and last time. The more you wonder, the more wonder-full everything becomes. Living wonder-fully will wake you up to today.

A WHOLE DAY

May you live all the days of your life.

Jonathan Swift

One of the very first creative growth games I devised for the Laughter Clinic was called, 'A Whole Day'. The aim of this delightful game is to live a whole day, 24 hours, with the 'soul' purpose of being and doing anything and everything that will help you and others to feel more whole, more loved and more fulfilled. For a whole day, your conscious purpose is wholeness, and your creative focus is the moment at hand.

What would you do, from dawn to dusk, with a whole day dedicated to wholeness? What a question! How would you begin the day? How would you fill each moment? Where would you go? What would you do? Whom would you see? Whom *wouldn't* you see? How would you think? What would you communicate? How would you dress? What would you eat? What *wouldn't* you eat? What would you give? One whole day of this creative, conscious living would be like a lifetime, an eternity!

Look to your diary now and set a date as soon as possible for creating 'A Whole Day' in your life. Life is a creative, conscious act. Consciousness grows, expands and evolves when you resolve to live for always in the moment. 'Every situation—nay, every moment—is of infinite worth, for it is the representative of a whole eternity,' wrote Johann von Goethe. Make your life momentous!

Here is an example of 'A Whole Day' I personally first imagined and then lived:

I will wake at dawn to see a sunrise.
I will thank God for Today.
I will pray for a friend.
I will send healing to the world.
I will give a compliment.
I will tell someone, 'I love You'.
I will smile more, to everyone.
I will make someone laugh.
I will sit with a flower.
I will walk with nature.
I will listen to a bird sing.
I will watch a cloud pass by.
I will forgive someone.
I will show kindness to someone.
I will say 'Thank you' to someone.
I will contact a forgotten friend.
I will look for something new.
I will listen to heavenly music.

I will smell jasmine.
I will eat a favourite food.
I will watch a star in the sky.
I will breathe with the wind.
I will thank God for today.
I will sleep, the whole night
through.

I hope this example may inspire you to imagine and to live a personal whole day of your own. Do not stop at one whole day. Have more! The real challenge of this creative growth game is to see how you can creatively, consciously make each of your todays a little more whole than your yesterdays.

'NOW OR NEVER'

Procrastination is the thief of time.

Edward Young

I have a brother, David, who is four years younger than me. I call him 'my favourite brother' simply because he is my only brother and I always like to make the best of any situation! As children, it had always been my brother's dream to share a house with me one day. 'Wouldn't it be great, Rob, if we could live together,' he would say. To be truthful, I did not share his enthusiasm; nor, however, did I share his remarkable vision, for David and I did eventually live together. Thought is creative!

'Can I come and stay with you in Birmingham for two weeks or so?' David asked during a phone call from Winchester one day. I was delighted at the idea. The 'two weeks or so' turned out to be nearly two years, during which time David actually bought my house off me. Once a landlord, I became a tenant in my own home! I was also cook, cleaner, washroom assistant, account keeper and gardener. It seems crazy now, but David has this amazing knack of getting everybody else to do things for him.

I gave David one chore: to put the milk bottle out each day! It soon became apparent that David was unable to find the time in his busy schedule to do even this task. After a week, he had seven milk bottles in a plastic bin liner in his bedroom. After two months, David had three full plastic bin liners with over 50 milk bottles all over the bedroom floor. 'I can't sleep,' he complained, 'The milk bottles clank in the night.' 'I hate my bedroom,' he protested. 'Can I come and sleep with you?' he pleaded. Procrastination had turned a simple chore into a macabre, black-comedy nightmare.

I once heard procrastination described as, 'the art of keeping up with yesterday'! The procrastinator always spends today dealing with yesterday. 'Soon', 'after', 'if only', 'if, when', 'but', 'then', tomorrow', 'later' and 'next time' are the common parlance of the procrastinator. Alas, procrastination and delay have never once in the history of humanity solved a problem; many a time, though, they have compounded a problem and made it even worse.

'Life, as it is called, is for most of us one long postponement,' wrote Henry Miller. It is true that most people are forever getting ready to live but never really living. It is as if most people are warming up for life, having a trial run, or simply waiting for the main event to begin. The news is...the show has already started! You are already in the middle of your starring role! Fear not that your life will end, fear that it might never begin.

The difference between empowerment and powerlessness is the difference between 'now' and 'never'. This moment, *now*, is the one time in your life that you can make your own. Life is happening now, so stop waiting to start living 'if', 'when' or 'after'. When you miss out on 'now' you miss out on life. Resolve not to let fear, anxiety or laziness rob you of the time of your life. 'Now' is the time of your life.

Decide to be a non-procrastinator. Set a date to live for ever now. Replace 'maybe' with 'yes', 'I'll see' with 'I can' and 'tomorrow' with 'today'. Affirm thoughts of courage and relax thoughts of fear. Strengthen your belief systems and discipline your behaviour. Substitute blame and excuses with responsibility and answers. Stop talking to people about what you will do; show them instead what you are doing.

Reward your Self for becoming a non-procrastinator. Celebrate your conclusions and your accomplishments. Treat your Self! You deserve all the Self-congratulation you can give to your Self, because by affirming that you are now a non-procrastinator you will at last be free to take responsibility for your life. The ultimate reward of non-procrastination is that you can start to enjoy your freedom 'now' and not 'later'.

THIS DAY

This day, I will make a day of it. Today, I
will enjoy my life as never before.

The time to make a difference to your life is now. The day to begin again and start over is today. Conscious–creative living is a challenge to make the most of every moment; it is inspired by the positive belief that every moment in life is here to encourage you to unfold, evolve and become your full, true Self. The truth is, every moment of this day has a design about it that will, ultimately, help to build your happiness, your fulfilment and your joy.

There is a gift wrapped up in every moment of time that is yours to make and yours to find. The quicker you are able to rise to the moment, the sooner you will be able to reflect upon a happier past and anticipate a brighter future. Truly, *the present is where the presents are.* Be present: learn from the past, look to the future but, above all, live for today. 'Every man's life lies within the present,' wrote Marcus Aurelius, 'for the past is spent and done with, and the future is uncertain.'

The following 'Today Affirmations' are a sequence of positive statements that affirm life in the present, at this moment. They have proved to be very useful for helping people to face the day with courage, creativity and a fresh consciousness. Once again, they are best practised by following the affirmation guidelines set out on page 60. The best 'Today Affirmations' are the ones you create for your Self.

Breathe in: *Affirm: 'Today is of infinite worth and value to me.'*

Breathe out: *See it. Feel it. Behave as if you believe it.* ***(Repeat three times)***

Breathe in: *Affirm: 'Today is the day to make the most of my life.'*

Breathe out: *See it. Feel it. Behave as if you believe it.* ***(Repeat three times)***

Breathe in: *Affirm: 'Today is my chance to be more loving than yesterday.'*

Breathe out: *See it. Feel it. Behave as if you believe it.* **(Repeat three times)**

Breathe in: *Affirm: 'Today is my chance to be more joyful than yesterday.'*

Breathe out: *See it. Feel it. Behave as if you believe it.* **(Repeat three times)**

Breathe in: *Affirm: 'Today is my chance to be more wonder-full than yesterday.'*

Breathe out: *See it. Feel it. Behave as if you believe it.* **(Repeat three times)**

Breathe in: *Affirm: 'Today is my chance to be more authentic than yesterday.'*

Breathe out: *See it. Feel it. Behave as if you believe it.* **(Repeat three times)**

Breathe in: *Affirm: 'Today is my chance to be more prosperous than yesterday.'*

Breathe out: *See it. Feel it. Behave as if you believe it.* **(Repeat three times)**

Breathe in: *Affirm: 'Today is my chance to be more harmonious than yesterday.'*

Breathe out: *See it. Feel it. Behave as if you believe it.* **(Repeat three times)**

Breathe in: *Affirm: 'Today is for living, for loving and for laughing.'*
Breathe out: *See it. Feel it. Behave as if you believe it.*
(Repeat three times)

Breathe in: *Affirm: 'Today is a miniature life all of its own—it is quite different to any other day.'*
Breathe out: *See it. Feel it. Behave as if you believe it.*
(Repeat three times)

Life is a chance! Every moment is an invitation to change, to evolve and to develop for the better. Make your chance; take your chance—today!

CELEBRATION

Live in wonder. Say in your heart, 'Today, I will celebrate'
and, surely, you will find something wonderful to celebrate.

Life is to be celebrated! To celebrate is a basic human need,
as important as love, laughter and lungs! Celebration, at its
highest, is a kind of worship: it is reverence, gratitude,
recognition and joy. An ability to celebrate is inspired,
above all, by the ability to wonder: *celebration is the highest
expression of conscious–creative day-to-day living.* Celebration
is living wonder-fully.

Celebration is proof of existence: it is a statement of
intent and a declaration of the will to live life, love life
and make the most of life. Celebration is, ultimately, *an
unconditional acceptance of life, expressed joyfully.* The
challenge of celebration, therefore, is to celebrate
everything, 'ups' and 'downs', 'smiles' and 'frowns', 'good'
and 'bad', 'happy' and 'sad'. Celebration is a purpose of life
and a lesson of life.

Celebration is acceptance and recognition that life
always goes your way—life is for you, not against you. Life
is how you take it: celebration encourages you to take it
that everything is here to help you, not harm you.

Celebration is natural because existence is essentially enjoyable. You are here on Earth to enjoy life! By making celebration the focus of your life, you will find more to celebrate in life.

When was the last time you celebrated being alive?

GIFTS

And could you keep your heart in wonder at the daily miracles of your life, your pain would not seem less wondrous than your joy.

Kahil Gibran, The Prophet

One of the most enriching creative growth games devised for the Laughter Clinic is called 'Celebration Meditation'. This enjoyable contemplation is inspired by two simple questions: first, at the beginning of the day, 'What will I do to celebrate life today?'; second, at the end of the day, 'How have I celebrated life today?' Celebration is a meditation. The more you celebrate, the more there is to celebrate.

Life is for your enrichment; *everybody and everything is here to help you evolve, unfold and fulfill your wonder-full Self!* The 'Celebration Meditation' teaches you that everything is, directly or indirectly, a gift. One particular friend of the Laughter Clinic, June, had the idea to enhance this lovely meditation by creating her own personal 'Celebration Diary' in which she records all her celebrations. 'This diary is the most important thing I own, for it reminds me, when I really need reminding, that I am truly blessed,' she once told me.

At the Laughter Clinic we have a motto: 'Celebration is

Celestial!' Life is a gift, and you are truly blessed. Every day is a gift, completely unique, and you are truly privileged to be a part of it. The fun of waking up is searching for the gift of today. Celebration is knowing that there is a gift to be had in everything if you can accept it. Every moment is a blossom in time; every event ripens you a little more; and every experience bears a fruit.

To celebrate is to give as well as to receive. Celebration is contribution; it is a way of paying your respect to life. What you *contribute* to life is your *tribute* to life. What will be your gift to life today? Who will receive your gift? Who will prosper because of you? What will you donate of your Self to the world? The ultimate gift, of course, is to give a portion of your Self—your real, authentic Self. Truth has always been the ultimate gift.

DIVINITY

> Celebrate!—you are divine; Celebrate!—you are immortal and you will outlive time.
>
> *Yogi Ananda*

'Every flower of the field, every fibre of a plant, every particle of an insect, carries with it the impress of its Maker, and can—if duly considered—read us lectures of ethics or divinity,' wrote Thomas Pope Blount. What beautiful words! You and I are product and custodian of the universal, creative Intelligence. Our highest purpose in life is to make conscious our universal, creative potential.

Celebrate who you are. Celebrate, now, who you aim to become. Your potential is divine. You are the world in miniature. The Spirit of the Universe dwells within you.

Celebration is the realization that you are supported by the universe and that you are, right at this moment, part of a universal sea of abundant courage, love, joy, inspiration, light and healing. It is written in the ancient Eastern contemplation, the *Chandogya Upanishad*,

> This is the Spirit that is in my heart, smaller than a grain of rice, or a grain of barley, or a grain of mustard-seed, or a grain of canary-seed, or the kernel of a grain of canary-seed. This is the Spirit that is in my heart, greater than the Earth, greater than the sky, greater than heaven itself, greater than all these worlds.

You need not pray to receive love, for you are already loved; you need not pray to receive bravery, for you are already brave; you need not pray for wisdom, for you are already wise. In fact, you need not pray for anything to come to you, for it is already here; pray instead that you might open your Self up, consciously and creatively, to allow and to accept. The gifts of the universe are already open to you—they are now waiting for you to open up to your Self!

Celebration is also the realization that as well as being supported by the universe you are also a complete, integral part of the universe. You are part of everything you see and everyone you meet. You, me and the universe are as One: we come from the same place, and one day, finally, we will arrive at the same place. To make a connection, to build a bridge, to make peace and to create harmony— these are the ultimate celebrations.

Celebration is also the realization that the authentic you, the real Self, is never born and never dies. Spirit is immortal. Death is not an end, it is transition. Just as winter creates spring, death creates life. Death is not a time for funereal sadness; death can be a celebration too, a tribute to life, immortal life. Let us live as if we are immortal; let us celebrate that we will always be, somewhere and somehow, a part of this wonder-full universe.

HEART

Celebration is a whole-hearted 'thank you' for the greatest gift of all: life!

Celebration is the song of creation: it is joy, it is love and it is courage. It is also life-affirming. To give whole-heartedly to life is the very best way to receive life. To live consciously–creatively from the heart, never missing an opportunity to love and be loved, is celebration enough for anyone. Celebration is a dedication; it is an act of devotion.

Celebration is a prayer; it is love in action. 'Love is the joy of the good, the wonder of the wise, the amazement of the gods,' wrote Plato. Celebration is wonder-full: it is the realization that both you and I are on this planet to learn how to love. Ask your Self, 'What can I do to love my Self more, today?' Then ask your Self, 'What more can I do radiate my love to others, today?' Life shines when we polish it with love.

Celebration is excitement—it is enthusiasm for life. Celebration inspires a whole-hearted response to life; it creates energy, enterprise, adventure, initiative and spirit. Celebration is also heart-felt gratitude for life: it is reverence, appreciation, wonder and praise. Celebration, enthusiasm and joy transform the ordinary into the extraordinary: they make the moment precious, for ever.

Another of the most popular creative growth games of the Laughter Clinic is called 'Devotions'. This exercise sets a joyful challenge: 'What will you devote your life to today?' Each and every day, decide to devote your Self to a theme, a thought, a cause, a belief—to love, laughter, kindness or praise, for instance. 'Devotions' is all about dedication, whole-heartedness and purposefulness—it inspires creative–conscious day-to-day living.

WONDER-FULL

To rejoice in the fullness of life is an act of
worship, a celebration divine.

Rolly Hughes

Living wonder-fully is a conscious–creative act of discovery, expression and growth—it is the ultimate celebration of life. Living wonder-fully is a beautiful work of art: it takes practice, courage, dedication, laughter and devotion. Every day is a stimulating mix of opportunity, chance, advantage, choice, occasion and surprise, and you are blessed with a wonder-full potential to make of it whatever you wish.

Living wonder-fully is a conscious–creative decision to say an unconditional 'Yes' to life—*all of life!* Wonder is a resolution to accept that life knows best and that, ultimately, everything that happens to you can be for the best. To put it another way, living wonder-fully is an awareness that you your Self have the power of conscious will and creative decision to bring out the best in any situation you face.

177

Living wonder-fully is a conscious–creative choice to live in harmony with life. We are peacemakers—we are here to help heal the pain, hurt, separation and suffering in this world, not because these things are 'wrong', but because we choose it is now time to integrate and transmute them. The Universal Creator does not intend for us to live in pain and suffering; our heritage is one of evolving joy, peace, happiness and wonder.

Living wonder-fully is also the happy realization that your fundamental aim in life is to enjoy your Self. You are here to discover your universal, creative potential for love, joy, happiness and growth. You are a beacon of light capable of illuminating the world with your life, your love and your laughter. Write it on your heart today: 'What a wonderful day it is', and then be brave enough to perceive it, think it, believe it, communicate it and act on it. In this way, your life will be wonder-full—and you will be an inspiration, an eternal memory, for all of us to savour and for us all to take with us.

Robert Holden is available to give workshops, seminars and lectures on Stress Busters, The Laughter Clinic Project and the psychology of Living Wonderfully. Details of Robert's 'Enjoyment in Employment' workshops, which include *Successful Stress Control, Time of Your Life* (Time Management), *Change for the Better* (Managing Change), *They're the Most Important Person on the Planet* (Customer Service) and *Team Spirit*, can also be received by writing to Robert c/o HarperCollins*Publishers*.

By the same author:

STRESS BUSTERS
Over 101 strategies for stress survival

Stress Busters is a creative, practical guide to successful
stress control—packed with effective coping strategies
for achieving positive health, personal happiness
and peak performance.
These include tips, tactics and techniques for:

deep relaxation • anxiety control • problem solving
• creative thinking • self-esteem • good health
• pain relief • better sleep • energy management
• happy relationships
and a host of other stress-related issues.

LAUGHTER, THE BEST MEDICINE
The healing power of happiness, humour and laughter

The healing properties of laughter have been acknowledged in the most ancient of cultures, from Greece to north-east Asia to South America. Today leading doctors are again recognizing the importance of laughter as an affective antidote to stress.

In *Laughter, The Best Medicine* Robert Holden shows how laughter should be valued as a basic need —as important as love and life itself—and he presents more than 50 of his most popular prescriptions for:

feeling good again • celebrating being alive
• enhancing love relationships
• releasing your 'fun child'
• embracing health and happiness
• profiting from fun and play at work
• improving your laughter-life
• enjoying new beginnings...Now!

Stress Busters	0 7225 2632 6	£6.99	☐
Laughter, The Best Medicine	0 7225 2827 2	£4.99	☐
What Number Are You?	1 85538 135 4	£5.99	☐
What Colour Are You?	0 85030 616 7	£4.99	☐
Your One–Week Way to Personal Success	0 7225 2599 0	£4.99	☐
Your One–Week Way to Mind Fitness	0 7225 2925 2	£4.99	☐
Superlife	0 7225 2600 8	£5.99	☐
Superlove	0 7225 2821 3	£5.99	☐

All these books are available from your local bookseller or can be ordered direct from the publishers.

To order direct just tick the titles you want and fill in the form below:

Name: _____

Address: _____

Postcode: _____

Send to: Thorsons Mail Order, Dept 3, HarperCollins*Publishers*, Westerhill Road, Bishopbriggs, Glasgow G64 2QT
Please enclose a cheque or postal order or your authority to debit your Visa/Access account

Credit card no: _____

Expiry date: _____

Signature: _____

to the value of the cover price plus:
UK & BFPO: Add £1.00 for the first book and 25p for each additional book ordered.
Overseas orders including Eire: Please add £2.95 service charge. Books will be sent by surface mail but quotes for airmail despatches will be given on request.

24 HOUR TELEPHONE ORDERING SERVICE FOR ACCESS/VISA CARDHOLDERS- 041 772 2281